The History of Ancient Rome
Part I

Professor Garrett G. Fagan

THE TEACHING COMPANY ®

PUBLISHED BY:

THE TEACHING COMPANY
4151 Lafayette Center Drive, Suite 100
Chantilly, Virginia 20151-1232
1-800-TEACH-12
Fax—703-378-3819
www.teach12.com

Garrett G. Fagan, Ph.D.

The Pennsylvania State University

Garrett G. Fagan was born in Dublin, Ireland and educated at Trinity College, Dublin. He received his Ph.D. from McMaster University, Hamilton, Ontario, and has held teaching positions at McMaster University, York University, University of North Carolina at Chapel Hill, Davidson College, and Penn State University. In all of these institutions, students rated his courses on the classical world as very good to excellent. He has also given numerous public lectures to audiences of all ages, including the Junior Classical League.

Professor Fagan has an extensive record of research in Roman social history and has held a prestigious Killam Postdoctoral Fellowship at the University of British Columbia, Vancouver. He has published articles in international journals, and his book on Roman public bathing culture was published by the University of Michigan Press in early 1999.

Table of Contents

The History of Ancient Rome
Part I

The History of Ancient Rome

Scope:

In the regional, restless, and shifting history of continental Europe, the Roman Empire stands as a towering monument to scale and stability; at its height, it stretched from Syria to Scotland, from the Atlantic Ocean to the Black Sea, and it stood for almost 700 years. So enormous was the Roman achievement in forging and maintaining this vast empire that the idea of Rome has left a lasting impression on the European psyche. Subsequent rulers from Charlemagne to Napoleon to Hitler were motivated to some degree by emulation of the Roman model, and if the modern movement to unify Europe under a single currency and guiding bureaucracy succeeds, it will be the first genuine and lasting realization of such emulation in 1400 years. Under Rome, people on three continents—in Europe, Africa, and Asia—gave their allegiance to a single political system, were governed by a unified set of laws, and were members of a distinct cultural community, despite their often profound linguistic, religious, and regional diversity. So grand was the power of the idea of Rome even in ancient times that the tribesmen who destroyed the Empire in the west often called themselves Romans, and Europe has seen some form of the Holy Roman Empire for most of its subsequent history. By no means insignificant also is the huge cultural debt that Europe and the world owe to Rome in so many fields of human endeavor, such as art, architecture, engineering, language, literature, law, and religion. In this series of lectures we examine how a small village of shepherds and farmers rose to be the colossus that bestrode the known civilized world of its day and came to leave such a lasting mark on European history.

After two introductory lectures on the value of studying ancient Rome and the nature of the historical evidence for antiquity, we focus in the following four lectures on the very earliest periods of Roman history. After examining the geopolitical and cultural shape of pre-Roman Italy, the foundation legends of Rome itself, and the cycle of stories that surrounds the kings of Rome, we pause to look at the shape of early Roman society. These topics offer excellent illustrations of the problems inherent in using ancient evidence for historical inquiry, which constitutes a running theme for the initial part of the course. Lectures Seven through 10 chart the fall of the monarchy at Rome and the foundation, in its wake, of the Republic (traditionally dated to 509 B.C.). The two major forces that influenced the shape of the early Republic, the Struggle of the Orders and Roman military expansion in Italy in the eighth to fourth centuries B.C., are treated, as is the means of Roman administration of conquered territories in Italy, which lay the foundations for the later acquisition and maintenance of the Empire.

Moving outside of Italy, Lectures 11 through 15 concern the rise of the Roman Empire in the third and second centuries B.C. Having examined the shape of the Mediterranean world prior to Rome's emergence onto the international scene, we devote two lectures to charting the course of the Romans' first two titanic struggles with their arch-rival in the west, Carthage. In these wars, the Romans first developed a large-scale navy, sent armies overseas, acquired foreign territories, and displayed what was to become one of their chief characteristics: a dogged determination to prevail, even in the face of seemingly impossible odds. This was particularly clearly brought out in the Second Punic War, when the gifted Carthaginian general Hannibal was abroad in Italy, threatening the very existence of Rome itself. Success in the first two Punic Wars set the stage for Roman expansion in the eastern Mediterranean, which brought Rome into conflict with the "superpowers" of the day. Following the outline of the facts of Roman overseas expansion, we seek explanations for it in Lecture Fifteen and thereby enter a field of heated scholarly debate.

Lectures 16 through 19 pause the narrative to examine two important thematic issues: the influence of Greek culture on Rome in the third and second centuries B.C., and the nature of the Roman Republican system of government in both the domestic and provincial spheres. This latter system—complex, tradition-bound, and replete with archaisms and redundancies—has influenced the form of several modern polities, including that of the United States. Finally, we examine the pressures of empire on Roman society, charting considerable social, economic, and political changes brought about by the speed and success of Rome's overseas expansion. For it was on the rocks of these pressures that the Republic was destined to founder.

The following eight lectures, 20 through 27, follow the course of what modern scholars have termed the "Roman Revolution." In the century between 133 and 31 B.C., the Roman Republic tore itself apart. It is a period of dramatic political and military developments, of ambitious generals challenging the authority of the state for their political development, of civil wars and vicious violence, and of some of the first great personalities of European history: Marius, Sulla, Pompey, and Julius Caesar. The story is intriguing, complicated, and at times horrendous, and it illustrates perfectly the historical principle of contingency. With a few exceptions, each protagonist in the drama of the Revolution tended to act within the bounds of necessity or precedent, and thereby to set new and dangerous precedents for later protagonists to follow. In this way, the Roman Revolution was not a staged or planned event, but a cumulative snowball of crises that combined to shatter the system of Republican government. By the time of Caesar's assassination in 44 B.C., few could have held any illusions as to the ultimate destination of the Roman body politic: autocracy.

After pausing to examine the social and cultural life of the Late Republic, we return in Lectures 29 and 30 to the very last phases of the Revolution and the rise to power of the man who was to become Rome's first Emperor, Augustus. Lectures 31 to 33 examine the long reign of Augustus (31 B.C.–A.D. 14) and his establishment of a new political order at Rome, called the Principate. His solution to the Republic's problems was clever and subtle, at once radically altering the nature of government while disguising that fact under a veneer of familiar Republican forms. The Principate stood for centuries and brought stability and good government, especially to the provinces, in a way that the old Republic had been incapable of doing. It also had a flaw at its core that made life for subsequent emperors and those close to them perilous indeed. This was the issue of the succession, how one emperor passed power onto the next. Engendered by Augustus' concealment of his autocracy under the forms of the old Republic, the problem of what happened when an emperor died was to prove the single most destabilizing factor in the Principate's existence.

Lectures 34 to 36 cover the early Imperial period, from the death of Augustus to the instability of the third century. This is the era of such familiar Roman historical figures as Caligula, Claudius, Nero, and Hadrian. Rather than treat each reign as a march of facts, we examine thematically, first, the gradual derailment of the pure Augustan Principate under his immediate successors and, second, the role of the emperor in general in the Roman world, citing examples to illustrate our points. Finally, we show how the problem of the succession combined with ominous developments among Rome's external enemies in the second and third centuries A.D. to generate a period of great crisis, indeed near-collapse, in the mid-third century A.D.

Leaving the Empire under pressure, we turn in Lectures 37 through 45 to consider some of the salient characteristics of classical Roman civilization. The selection of themes is, by necessity, limited and some omissions are unavoidable, but it addresses many topics of greatest interest to the modern historian investigating ancient Rome. Individual lectures are devoted to the broad shape of Roman society, slavery, the Roman family, the role of women in Roman society, urbanism, public leisure and mass entertainment, paganism, and the rise of Christianity.

To conclude the course, Lectures 46 through 48 return to the Empire's last centuries. We see the Empire restored to order and stability at the end of the third century, but under an increasingly oppressive and militarized government. The institutionalization of Christianity as the legitimation for imperial power and the more openly autocratic regime created, in many ways, a Roman Empire closer to medieval Europe than to the Empire of Augustus. As such, the later Empire is treated only in general terms here, since it warrants closer study in and of itself. We end the course with one of the great questions in history—why did the Roman Empire fall?— and we see how, in the eyes of most modern scholars, the Empire did not fall at all but just changed into something very different.

Lecture One
Introduction

Scope:

We introduce the course by asking why we should study ancient Rome at all and by considering the nature of ancient historical inquiry. The enormously rich heritage of ancient Rome to the modern world—in the spheres of language, art, literature, engineering, architecture, and government, to name but a few—more than justifies the study of the ancient fountainhead. Images and themes derived from or rooted in ancient Rome continue to exert an influence on the modern mind. In addition, unlike many ancient states, Rome changed hugely in many spheres over the course of its 1500-year history, and thus the history of Rome is an engaging, complex, and challenging subject. We will set the thematic, chronological, and geographical parameters of the course. Finally, we turn to the nature of ancient history and examine how it differs in means and method from what most people consider "typical" history.

Outline

I. Why study ancient Rome at all?

    A. The heritage of ancient Rome is enormous.

        1. The influence that Rome exerted on later ages, as illustrated by the "Grand Tours" that were conducted from the Renaissance through the 19th century, has been both profound and continuous.

        2. The Roman legacy to the modern world in various spheres is inestimable.

        3. From Rome, we have inherited, among other things, a reverence for the law. Certainly Rome influenced the Founding Fathers of the United States.

        4. The Roman Catholic Church is the manifestation of Rome in the modern world.

    B. The images and themes of Roman history and culture continue to influence modern culture. Rome's is an interesting history to study, due to patterns of change.

        1. Modern popular culture remains enthralled by images and themes drawn from the pagan Roman world: Julius Caesar assassinated, Nero fiddling as Rome burns, and gladiators fighting to the death before clamoring crowds.

> **2.** Roman society changed enormously over its long duration: it evolved from a monarchy into a republic, and then back to a monarchy; it changed from a pagan to a Christian empire; and culturally it evolved from a rustic and crude place to a sophisticated and Hellenized one.
>
> **3.** The long period of Rome's survival, coupled with the processes of change, make Rome's history more dynamic and variegated than that of any other ancient state and quite a few subsequent ones.

II. Introducing the course and setting parameters.

> **A.** This series of lectures will outline the main events of Roman history in the political, military, and social spheres. Some attention will also be paid to cultural matters where pertinent.
>
> **B.** By "ancient Rome" we mean the period from ca. 1000 B.C. to A.D. 500. The course focuses especially on the period c. 300 B.C. to A.D. 300. Late Antiquity (c. A.D. 300–500) is treated only briefly, and the Byzantine period (c. A.D. 300–A.D. 1453), not at all; both are deserving of courses in their own right.
>
> (* See note at end of Lecture One outline)
>
> **C.** In geographic terms, we shall examine Rome's expansion from a small hamlet on a hillside overlooking the Tiber River to the colossus that dominated the Mediterranean basin and northwestern Europe for a half a millennium.

III. Ancient history is not like modern history, which most people conceive of as "typical" history.

> **A.** History is, typically, a combination of facts about the past and the interpretation of those facts. Ancient history is somewhat different from modern history in several areas.
>
> **B.** The problem of evidence.
>
> > **1.** Unlike modern history, ancient history suffers from a relative dearth of evidence.
> >
> > **2.** The body of ancient evidence available to us is finite, well-known, patchy, and often contradictory.
> >
> > **3.** This makes the establishment of basic facts a more difficult endeavor than it is in modern history.

C. The scope of interpretation.
  1. Due to the scarcity of evidence, the scope for interpretation is extremely wide in ancient history.
  2. The circumscribed body of ancient evidence is itself subject to constant reevaluation and interpretation.
D. The absence of certainty.
  1. All of these circumstances make certainty a "rare bird" in ancient history.
  2. More often there are merely competing reconstructions and interpretations, with no clear way to decide among them.
  3. There are few "correct" answers to problems in ancient history; that is precisely what makes it so fascinating and exciting an endeavor.

Recommended Reading:

R. Jenkyns (ed.), *The Legacy of Rome: A New Appraisal.*

Supplemental Reading:

E. H. Carr, *What is History?*, 2nd edition.

M. I. Finley, *Ancient History: Evidence and Models.*

Questions to Consider:

1. Is it possible that, in fact, Rome never "fell" at all, in the sense that the idea of Rome has stood consistently behind so much of subsequent European and world history?

2. To what extent does the study of ancient history differ in its objectives and methods from the study of modern history? Can you account for those differences?

---

* *Erratum*: On the tape, the professor states that the Byzantine Empire fell in A.D. 1454. The correct date is A.D. 1453, as shown in the outline.

Introduction

Welcome to The Teaching Company's course on The History of Ancient Rome. My name is Garret Fagan, from the Pennsylvania State University, where I teach Latin, Roman History and Roman Civilization. I will be your guide for the next 48 lectures, as we survey the sprawling, majestic, complex (I will be straightforward and say that up front) and occasionally somewhat frightening history of the longest lived and largest empire mainland Europe has seen.

For this and the next lecture, before we embark on the details of the history of Rome, I want to introduce you to the subject, address some very basic issues and, in this, the first lecture, and in the next lecture, introduce you to the nature of the evidence for ancient history. To begin with, I think that we should start at the beginning and answer a question that has always been asked of me, "Why bother?" Why bother studying the history of ancient Rome? Then, we will look at the parameters of the course; we will set the limits of our study, the thematic, chronological, and geographic focuses of the course. Then I want to end this lecture with some personal thoughts specifically on the nature of ancient history and how it differs from what most people in the public consider to be typical history. That is the outline of this lecture.

First, why study ancient Rome at all? I am often asked that, most recently about three days ago. Someone said, "What do you do?" I said, "I teach ancient history." "Why?" It pays well isn't really the good answer. What is the reason for studying the ancient world and specifically Rome? I believe the answer to that is quite complicated. Again, it is a very personal answer. Different people will give you different answers to this question. I think the overwhelming reason is that Rome has exerted a continuous and profound influence on the history of not just Europe, but of the Western world, and because of the dominance of the Western world in the global forum of the whole world.

The heritage of ancient Rome is vast. I will give you just one example from the complicated mosaic of how this heritage has been transferred to us. This is the Grand Tour that was very popular from the Renaissance right through to the 19th century. It was especially popular amongst British noble-youths, especially noblemen, in the

18th century. The Grand Tour was a prerequisite for the educated man who had already read his Latin and Greek in school and perhaps in universities. The Grand Tour involved traveling over to the continent from England, usually beginning at Paris, and then with most an itinerary moving through the great cultural centers of Europe. The destination was invariably Rome. You could add in Florence and Naples, because in the 18th century at this time Pompeii was just being discovered and excavated in a very systematic way. So, Naples was also a popular destination, but for Roman reasons. Venice was also a popular spot. But, the ultimate destination was invariably Rome.

At any one time, there could be hundreds of Englishmen traversing the continent on their way to looking at all the ancient monuments. In 1786, for instance, Sir John Fleming Lester noted that Rome was "perfectly filled with Englishmen." Edward Gibbon was prompted to write his vast and magisterial study *The Decline and Fall of the Roman Empire* while sitting on the Capitoline Hill in Rome, on the Grand Tour as a young man in 1764.

The direct way that the ancient world came into the modern through these Grand Tours is self-evident. When these people came back from Italy and Rome, they brought with them the sensibilities of the ancient world. They liked to decorate their houses, or build them even, in neoclassical styles. They liked to surround themselves either with genuine ancient artifacts or with fakes. In the poetry they wrote, the literature they wrote, they reproduced ancient Roman sensibilities again and again, direct cultural influence through the Grand Tour. That is only one tiny tessera of the grand mosaic. If we look around us in the modern world, the face of Rome is everywhere to be seen as long as you know where to look and how to identify it when you look there.

First, the Romans have given us two major models of government: a balanced republic using a limited and franchised body of citizens who elect members of a council that has an executive branch of officers answerable to that council, who carry out the orders of that council. That is a Roman model of government. The other model, which is not popular on this side of the Atlantic but which has been very popular in Europe and is still around in certain places, is a monarchy, but it is a monarchy tempered by law and tradition, and a monarchy answerable to councils and the public. Another form of government that has died out since, but was very popular and common in Europe for many centuries, was absolute monarchy. All of these are Roman models.

In the case of the United States of America, for instance, the founders were unequivocally and directly influenced by their knowledge of the ancient Roman past in formulating the Constitution. Recent books have emerged that bring this out absolutely clearly. One published in 1995 was called *The Founders and the Classics.* So it is not just the polity of the USA that has been influenced by ancient Rome but how the attitudes toward pastoralism, agriculture, the place of the citizen in the state, and so forth, were all informed by the founders' knowledge of the classics and particularly of the Roman classics.

Another feature of the Roman world that we inherited and take for granted is our reverence for the law. The Romans loved the law. They conceived of the law somewhat differently from the way we do. It wasn't the law of individual human rights the way our modern law is, but the notion that the law stands above us all, that the law is something to which all of us are answerable including the members of the government, that is a Roman concept. The Romans also were very profligate by ancient standards with their citizenship, which is another feature of America if we think about it. Many people can come and become citizens of America. The notion of a universal citizenship is a Roman notion. We could say in all fairness that the very notion of the West is founded on a memory of ancient Rome. Europe has almost always seen, until the last century, some form of the Holy Roman Empire, although in Voltaire's words, it was neither Holy, nor Roman, nor an Empire. The very idea that people would call a political entity in Europe a "Roman Empire," shows the power of the memory of Rome, which I think arguably stands at the foundation of our concept of the West as a cultural and political entity.

In more everyday ways, we see Rome all around us, in our art and architecture, especially large public buildings. The Capitol in Washington comes immediately to mind. This is a Roman building. Some people may think it is Greek, but they are speaking from architectural ignorance. This is Roman. The Greeks didn't have domes. Romans were the ones who developed concrete and so, were able to develop curvilinear forms of architecture which were encased in Greek classical forms (columns and marble and so forth.) However, this is very much a neoclassical, but very much a Roman model of public architecture. If you look at ancient Roman temples and compare them to, say, the Supreme Court building, the influence is crystal clear and does not need to be built upon. If we take a very specific form of Roman building, the triumphal arch, which was really a monument of personal egotism, built by successful generals and eventually emperors, then look at the Arc de Triomphe in Paris, one of the major monuments of Paris built by an egoistic individual, we can see that the architectural and artistic heritage continues. This is just in the form of architecture. I haven't mentioned painting, sculpture and so forth, all of which have governed, or at least greatly exercised, an influence on the forms of Western art and cultural achievement.

By far, the most direct descendant of ancient Rome is the Catholic Church, because the Catholic Church is in many ways the son of Rome. It is the Roman Empire made manifest in the modern world. It has an absolute emperor in the form of the pope. The pope is called the Supreme Pontiff. Why? Have you ever wondered why he is called the Supreme Pontiff? That is because the ancient Roman chief priest was called the *Pontifex Maximus*, which means the Supreme Pontiff. Why? That is a different matter. It may be that we get to that when we look at Roman paganism later in the course. The very title and nature of the papacy is modeled on the Roman Empire. Where does the pope live? He lives in Rome. He lives in Rome surrounded by neoclassical buildings. He has around him a council of cardinals. Like ancient emperors who would send out governors to the provinces, he sends out to cardinals to govern specific regions of the Catholic world. Those governors have under them a series of underlings going down to the parish priest who help them administer the Catholic world. This resemblance between the Roman Empire and the Catholic world is not coincidence. As we will see later in the course when we look at the rise of Christianity, one of the reasons for the success of the Christian church was precisely its conscious modeling of its organization on the secular Roman government of the Empire.

So much for some of the influences. I have just scratched the surface, and there are many more that we can talk about which have come down to us from the ancient world, and specifically from ancient Rome. There are other reasons I think it is worth studying Roman history. There is no doubt that in the popular image, there are certain powerful themes, images in the mind that can spring to mind when one thinks of ancient Rome and that still resonate with us: Caesar murdered when he comes into the Senate house, Nero fiddling while Rome burns, gladiators fighting to the death on the sand in front of ravening crowds, chariot races, decadence and orgies. These are all images that come to mind of ancient Rome, and they can be found reproduced in popular culture either directly or indirectly again and again. I recently heard an excellent paper that showed that themes drawn from Roman history have infused many science fiction TV and movie depictions, particularly the images of bread and circuses, the notion of manipulative government that keeps the population docile through violent entertainment. It is in various *Star Trek* episodes and movies like *Roller Ball* and so forth. These are all themes that are familiar to us that can be rehoused, recast, and represented to us in recent science fiction, but they are all drawn from the Roman world.

There is another more mundane reason for studying Roman history. That is that it's just really interesting. The Roman Empire was extremely large. It stretched from Syria to Scotland, from the Black Sea to the Atlantic Ocean, spanning three continents. It was extremely long-lived as empires go—500 years, which is quite a remarkable achievement—how the empire survived so long. More than anything else, during that long period, over that great expanse of land, it changed enormously. Unlike many ancient states which tended to be fairly static, the Roman Empire changed socially, politically, culturally, again and again. It reinvented itself (to use a modern term) repeatedly. It changed from being a monarchy to being a republic back to a monarchy and ultimately to being a divinely legitimated monarchy on the model of the medieval monarchy. Just that political process is fascinating to trace, the way the Romans adapted and changed themselves to fit the new circumstances. Culturally, it changed from a basic, rustic, simple society to a highly sophisticated urbanized, Hellenized society. By Hellenized, I mean influenced by the Greeks, and we will be looking at that in some detail later in the course. So, the long period of Rome's survival, when coupled with the success of the empire and the way it changed over times makes the study of ancient Rome a very interesting and fascinating subject in and of itself.

I hope that answers the question "Why?" I have just advanced some personal reasons why I believe that the study of the ancient world is so valuable and the study of ancient Rome in particular. What I want to do now is to set the parameters of the course, to focus on what we will be looking at, and just as importantly what we will not be looking at over the course of the coming lectures. When you do the history of any subject, especially one as vast as ancient Rome (we are covering maybe 1500 years of history here) there are so many things that could be looked at that we are going to have to "cut-and-paste," if you like, and focus on certain things to the detriment of others. I believe that the political and military history of Rome is the core of the subject, and we will be looking at that in no uncertain way. We will be focusing on the development of the Roman state along the lines I have just mentioned, and we will be looking at the rise, maintenance, and eventually the fall of the Roman Empire in the West. We will also look at some of what can be broadly described as social historical issues. What was Roman society like? What was it like to live there? What were the Roman's social attitudes like? What were their families like? Why did they have slaves and what was the life of the slave like? What did they do for entertainment and relaxation? What were their religious beliefs like? Why did Christianity emerge as the dominant religion of the Roman Empire? Under what circumstances did that happen? After years of persecution, how did Christianity emerge out of the roiling mass of religions that made up the Roman Empire? Those sorts of social historical issues are those that we will be looking at as well.

What we will not be looking at, unfortunately, are artistic and cultural matters in any great detail. I have just talked about Roman architecture and its influence on monumental, especially public, secular architecture of the modern era. That is something that we will not have time to look at. It is really a subject in and of itself, a course of Roman art history would be something that could occupy 48 lectures without any difficulty. Likewise, we won't have much time to look at literary matters. The rise, development and nature of Roman literature are not things that we'll look at in detail. We will have to address authors; we will look at certain authors who were important for historical reasons and as sources for the ancient world, but we will not examine the course of Roman literature, the history of Roman literature in and of itself. That is something we have to leave to the side. So, that and similar issues, cultural issues, really are something that we will perfunctorily look at but won't examine in any detail.

In terms of chronological parameters, what are we going to say of chronological limits on the course. Technically ancient Rome starts around 1000 B.C., and technically, if we include the Byzantine Empire, which includes the Eastern Roman Empire which survived after the fall of the Western Empire, it technically ends in A.D. 1454 [sic 1453]. We are not going to cover all that territory. It would simply be impossible. The main focus of the course will be up to the collapse of the Roman Empire in the West, which is traditionally dated to A.D. 476. I will be even more specific. We will actually be focused on what is often called the central period of Roman history, the period that focuses from 300 B.C. to A.D. 300. The reason I am setting those limits is that the study of late antiquity of the period of the Christianized Roman Empire is an immensely complicated one, and it is worthy of a course in and of itself. In the view of many modern scholars, late antiquity bleeds into medieval Europe. We are not going to take the story down to the medieval period. So, our chronological limits will be roughly focusing on the period 300 B.C. to A.D. 300. We will look at the early Roman period. I will cover the issue of late antiquity and the fall of the Roman Empire, but I will do so in less detail than I will the central core period of classical Roman history.

In geographical terms we will follow the rise of the Roman Empire from a small hamlet of shepherd huts overlooking the River Tiber in Italy to a colossus that bestrode the then known civilized world. Our geographic parameters will basically be dictated by the activities of the Romans themselves, which were really quite energetic, as we will see.

I want to end the lecture with some very personal thoughts on the nature of ancient history, and to introduce the themes, methods and approaches of ancient historical research, which in the view of many differ in significant ways from what most people consider typical history. If one were to be guided by what history is by looking at television, one would be convinced that history is Hitler, basically, because he seems to show up every time there is a history show. We get Hitler, or World War II, or generally more recent events. It is not hard to see why. Television requires moving pictures, and it is only in the more recent history that we have those available to us. The study of modern history is one that has a very set quorum of methods to it. Ancient history shares many of those methods with modern history, but with some significant differences. First, to make a sweeping generalization, what is history? History is, broadly speaking, a two-part process. It is the assemblage of facts about the past. That is part one. Part two is the interpretation of those facts. It is all good and well to know that the Battle on the Somme started on July 1, 1916. What is the meaning of the Battle on the Somme? Why is it important? Why should we know that? Why should we look at it at all? That is the issue of interpretation.

Ancient history is, like all history pretty much in its broad outline, in that shape. You assemble facts, and you try to interpret them. The biggest difference between ancient history and the study of more recent periods is the problem of the evidence. I am going to devote the whole next lecture to the issue of what the ancient evidence is. Right now, let me introduce you to the problem and outline the sorts of limits it places on our knowledge and the way ancient history is done.

If you were to attempt to write a history of the U.S. Congress as a single individual in which you incorporated the development of the physical environment in which the Congress appeared, the constitution of the Congress, every statue that was ever put out by the Congress it its history, the relationship of the Congress to every president who has ever been sitting, the various influential, individual Congressmen and Senators who have sat—at one time or another—in the U.S. Congress, you would be facing an impossible task. The volume of material you would have available to you would make it impossible for one person to do that. Because, in the ancient world, there is a limited body of material, it is possible to write a book with the title *The Senate of Imperial Rome* or *The Magistrates of the Roman Republic* covering maybe 500 years of history in a single or two-volume work. It is possible for one person to master the evidence because there is a limited body of ancient data. That is the single greatest difference between the study of ancient history and the study of more recent periods. The body of ancient material is finite. It is mostly pretty well-known. It has been known for most of its history (at least for most of the history of scholarship on the ancient world). It is also patchy and often contradictory. This makes the study of the ancient world a very difficult and challenging business.

I will give you an example. It is estimated that of all the literature that was written by the Greeks and Romans combined, of all the stuff that was originally out there—maybe in the library of Alexandria or the great libraries in Rome—of all that material, less than five percent has survived. We have less then five percent of the literature that was originally out there. We have authors that we don't even know existed. We have authors that we know the names of, we might know what they wrote about, but we don't know anything else about. Some authors survive almost entirely. For some authors various percentages of their work survive completely, or they survive in summaries written by later writers. It is a patchy, shifting body of material. It is very difficult to master it. I have heard it said (I really like this analogy and can't remember where I came across it) that studying the ancient world is like looking into the palace at Versailles through keyholes. You are able to see certain things extremely clearly. Other things are a little blurry, and there are whole wings that you simply can't see. There are whole floors, wings and levels of the palace that we can't see. There are areas of the ancient world that are inaccessible to us by the nature of the evidence that we have presented to us or that has survived over the intervening centuries.

This makes the establishment of the facts in ancient history much more difficult than in more modern periods. No one really doubts that the Second World War started when it did. People know the exact minute that John F. Kennedy finally passed away and so on. Establishing facts like that in the ancient world and in the study of Rome is often very difficult. We do know that Caesar was killed on the 15th of March in 44 B.C. Other things are far less clear to us. The order of events is often a matter of tremendous debate. To take an example, the issue of the breakout of the second Punic war, which we look at in more detail later in the course, is a matter of some discussion. This was a war that almost eliminated Rome from the face of the planet, because the Carthaginian was a man called Hannibal. This war started in Spain, and it started over a dispute about a rather inconsequential place in Spain called Saguntum. It is a matter of tremendous debate over the nature of Roman/Carthaginian relations in the lead up to the dispute over Saguntum. What was the nature of the agreement about the spheres of influence in Spain between Rome and Carthage? When was that agreement reached? Where did Saguntum fit into that agreement? When did the Romans establish a friendship with Saguntum that allowed them ultimately to side with this place and start a war with Carthage? Not that the Romans started the war, but it was the spark that ignited this massive conflict. All of those basic facts, fundamental facts, as to the start of this titanic struggle between these great states, are all matters of debate. They are not matters of certainty.

This leads us to the next major facet of ancient historical inquiry. That is, because of the limited body of evidence, the scope of interpretation by modern scholars is far broader for the study of the ancient world than it is for the modern. I am not saying that modern historians are all in one big happy agreement sitting around in a rose garden, eating lollypops and saying how they all agree with each other. It is far from it; of course they are not. But, the sorts of things that they argue about are so much more marginal by the values of the ancient historian that there is a big difference there. Interpretation in the study of the ancient world is far broader than it is for the study of the modern world. This leads to what I have termed "the absence of certainty." As I have said, there are certain things that we know. Remember the keyhole image. We can see through the keyhole into certain parts of the palace, but there are whole areas of the palace that we can't see. Certainty is very much the rare bird of the study of ancient Rome. There are certain things that we can absolutely say with confidence if the ancient evidence is focused on those things. (Again, I am leading into the next lecture here a little bit.) This is what we will be seeing the next time around.

More often than not, what you have in the study and history of ancient Rome are competing reconstructions, models, to explain the events that we have preserved for us in the ancient evidence. This means there are few definitely correct answers that can be given to very many fairly fundamental questions about the facts of the ancient Roman world. I don't want to over simplify here, but there are certainly issues that remain a matter of tremendous discussion and debate—fundamental issues that are forced upon the modern ancient historian looking at the ancient world by the nature of the evidence. Primary evidence is what we are coming back to again and again. That is what we are going to look at in the next lecture.

Lecture Two
The Sources

Scope:

All history, and especially ancient history, is founded on knowledge and use of the "primary sources," i.e., those sources that derive directly from the period under study. Before embarking on our survey of ancient Roman history, it is advisable to assess the sorts of evidence that we have available to us from the ancient world. Those sources divide into archaeological (physical) evidence and written evidence. We will discuss, with examples, the relative merits and limitations of each type.

Outline

I. History is based on the "primary sources."

    A. Primary sources are those sources that derive directly from the period under study.

        1. "Primary sources" can vary in quality and focus, and they can sometimes be removed from their subjects by some distance. Whatever the case, they hail from the cultural ethos of the ancient world.

        2. "Secondary sources," in contrast, are works of modern scholarship about the ancient past.

        3. All secondary sources are grounded in the primary sources.

    B. Historical theorists have argued at length about the relative merits of primary sources.

        1. One view, called "positivism," says that one can never go beyond what the primary sources tell us.

        2. "New History" holds to the view that the primary evidence can be supplemented by comparative and theoretical data drawn from other realms of scholarship. The inherent bias of the practicing historian can be minimized and the past "reality" can be reconstructed by close attention to the original context of the primary evidence. This is history "from the bottom up."

3. "Postmodernists" argue that there is no reality beyond the text. The inherent bias of the historian cannot be overcome and, in fact, history is not "reconstructed" but merely "constructed" in the image of the historian's biases.
4. In this series of lectures we shall take a broadly modernist approach, while acknowledging the warnings of the "postmodernists" about the depth of one's own bias.

II. Archaeological evidence comprises any and all physical material that survives from antiquity.

A. At just over 100 years old, "scientific" archaeology is a new discipline and has turned up a variety of physical evidence for our consideration.
1. "Macro" evidence comprises such artifacts as entire cities, buildings, infrastructures, ships, works of art, corpses, and so on.
2. "Micro" evidence offers fragments of pots, bones, textiles, and other small items, and even pollen and micro-organisms.
3. Pottery is a very common and important type of archaeological evidence.

B. Archaeological excavation is destructive, and the evidence it produces is mute and only "speaks" when interpreted.

III. Written evidence offers unparalleled insights into the lives of the ancients.

A. Ancient literature is rich and varied, and it is an invaluable historical tool.
1. The surviving body of Roman literature comprises many genres.
2. Classical literature gives us windows into ancient life as lived by the ancients, into their values and preoccupations, the main events of their history, and their own view of themselves.
3. Ancient literature mostly survives in medieval copies and is therefore a selected body of material subject to loss or the introduction of error in the process of copying.

B. Epigraphic evidence comprises inscriptions with varied content carved on a variety of surfaces.

    1. Inscriptions can be carved on stone, metal, bone, wood, bark, parchment, or papyrus.

    2. They include epitaphs, decrees, laws, commemorative and honorary texts, letters, notes, records, and graffiti.

    3. Unlike literary evidence, epigraphic evidence has not been selected or copied over the centuries but speaks to us directly from antiquity.

C. Ancient written evidence has its limitations.

    1. Roman literature was written by upper-class men, who mostly lived at Rome, between c. 200 B.C. and A.D. 200.

    2. Inscriptions are largely formulaic and for the most part not particularly informative for the major events of Roman history.

D. The study of coins (numismatics) and papyrus (papyrology) are two important subfields in the investigation of ancient evidence.

    1. Roman coins are both archaeological and epigraphic artifacts, in that they can be studied from both perspectives.

    2. Papyrus is a particular kind of inscriptional source, often presenting detailed portraits of life at the local level.

Essential Reading:

M. Crawford (ed.), *Sources for Ancient History.*

Supplemental Reading:

M. I. Finley, *Ancient History: Evidence and Models.*

L. Keppie, *Understanding Roman Inscriptions.*

Questions to Consider:

1. Can the practicing historian ever overcome the bias ingrained by the social, cultural, and historical context in which that historian is operating? If so, how? If not, why not?

2. Are some classes of ancient evidence more trustworthy relative to others? If so, why?

Lecture Two—Transcript
The Sources

Hello and welcome to the second lecture in The History of Rome for The Teaching Company. This is the second of the introductory lectures, and I want to pick up where I left off last time where I was discussing the nature of ancient history and I stressed at the end of the last lecture the importance of the ancient evidence and how the limited, finite nature of the ancient evidence defines the whole discipline of the study of the ancient world. What I want to do in this lecture is expand on that theme and outline in some detail the nature of the ancient materials. I also want to outline some approaches, different approaches that have been adopted over the years by modern scholars using this ancient material.

All history is based on what are called primary sources. The primary sources can be broadly defined as those that derive from the period under study. They can vary in terms of their focus and their quality. In periods as long as the period of Rome, they can be far removed from the period they are writing about. We can have the likes of Plutarch, a Greek and Roman of the second century A.D., writing about King Romulus who lived 900 years previously. So, the question could be asked to what extent is he a primary resource at all? What does he know about Romulus? That is a good question, and the point in defense of classifying Plutarch no matter what he is writing about in the ancient world as a primary source is that he is a member of the ancient world. He is an ancient Roman who thought, lived and experienced antiquity in a way that no amount of research by a modern scholar such as myself could ever hope to replicate. So, the primary sources in the broadest definition are those sources that derive from the period under study even if they are focusing on eras or subjects far removed chronologically from the lifetime of the author in question.

If we have primary sources, you won't be surprised to hear that we also have secondary sources. Secondary sources are modern works, works by modern scholars who are reconstructing, assembling and interpreting the ancient data to write on a subject such as the Senate of imperial Rome or the life of Julius Caesar or whatever. It is important to stress that these sources are literally secondary. They are all grounded in the primary evidence. If there were no primary or ancient evidence, there would be no secondary scholarship. Before looking at the nature of the primary sources, I believe it is important to assess quickly some of the different approaches that have been taken to interpreting the ancient data over the years. Looking particularly at history writing, the writing of ancient history as an art, or as some might argue as a science. In its original form, history writing was more an act of literature. This is how it was for the ancients themselves. They were concerned to find out the truth about the past, their own and that of whomever they were studying. Their works of history were really works of literature. This tradition was very long lived, up to and including I would suggest Edward Gibbon and *The Fall of the Roman Empire* which can be studied as much today as a work of literature as a work of history. It is a good work of history, but it is very literary in its approach.

In the course of the 19th century, especially in Germany, history became more "scientific," and I used quotation marks there because there is a big question as to whether history is scientific at all or whether it is just an art form. In the 19th century, historians, especially historians of Rome, began to take a more scientific approach to the study of the past. They broadly emerged an approach that has been called "Positivism." Positivism is the assembling of every available piece of ancient data about the subject under study.

It is no coincidence that it is at this very period in the 19th century that the great collections of Latin inscriptions began. Some of them are still ongoing. The assembling of every Latin inscription that we know about gradually has been published over the years since the 19th century because the Positivists demand that all the evidence be readily available and at hand. Their job is to assemble every piece of data concerning the subject that they want to study, and then presenting that in gargantuan footnotes usually along with their various interpretations and the interpretations of other scholars with whom they're disputing or agreeing or whatever the case may be. The Positivist view is fundamentally that we cannot step beyond the boundaries of the ancient evidence. If we revert to our model of the palace at Versailles, all we can write about is what we can see. If there are wings of the ancient past, the palace of the ancient past that we can't see, then we can't see them. We have to accept them and move on. Positivism was extremely successful in establishing an awful lot of information about the ancient past, especially when it was focused on the things that the ancient sources are interested in—namely politics and military matters. As long as you were studying the wars of the Romans or the development of the Roman Republic you had lots of information available to you. So, the Positivistic exercise was very successful for many years, for many decades, and in fact, in some quarters it is still ongoing.

In the 20th century, particularly since World War II, a new branch of history emerged, and it can't really be classified in any simple way. I've just termed it "New History." The New History was concerned with writing history from the bottom up. The New History said if there was a Roman Empire, and we would be looking at the politics and military endeavors of the Romans, we were looking at a minute fraction of the Roman Empire. What is everyone else doing? What are the farmers doing? What is the life of the slave like? What about the woman who is kept indoors? What about the marginalized brigands of Roman society? What about the people who the sources don't write about directly, but who show up from time to time, they are alluded to, they show up in anecdotes or are assumed to exist and may be assumed to be present in the room? For instance, a slave is assumed to be there at an ancient description of a dinner party. What was the dinner party like from the slaves' perspectives rather than from that of the people who are eating the food? This is the sort of question that New Historians (the historians from the bottom up) like to ask. When they came across to trying to investigate these subjects, they did not have much evidence. The ancients only wrote about what interested the upper classes, which we will see is where most of the literature for the ancient world derived from.

So, what do they do? They fill out the whole picture. They say if we can't see whole wings of the Palace of Versailles, let's look at other palaces we do know about and try to extrapolate. Let's look at comparative data. If we are studying slaving societies, what do other slaves in other societies feel about their condition? If we have nothing about the ancient Roman slave actually written down, what do other slaves think? We have information from the Antebellum South, from slaves in Brazil, and so forth. Let's use that. They use sociological and social scientific theory to fill out the picture— anthropological theory, anthropological analysis of cultures and societies to help fill out the gaps in the ancient evidence. This approach has been extremely successful. I'd like to read you a quote from one of its best proponents though he wasn't an ancient historian; he was an historian of modern England, but writes, I think, the best single sentence that summarizes this approach of history from the bottom up and the whole thesis of it. I refer to E.P. Thomson, a writer of British history who in his classic historical work *The Making of the English Working Class,* published in 1968, writes "I am seeking to rescue the poor stockinger, the ludite cropper, the obsolete hand-loom weaver, the utopian artisan, and even the deluded follower of Joanna Southcott from the enormous condescension of posterity." This is the attitude of New History summarized in a nutshell. You could say, "I am seeking to rescue the slave, the freed man, the brigand, the poor small holder of the Roman Republic from the enormous condescension of posterity." The exact same mentality is applied in the study of the ancient past for the new historians who focus on antiquity.

So, we have Positivists, and we have the New Historians. The most recent and most controversial approach is that adopted by Post-Modernists. The Post-Modernist movement as far as history is concerned really stems out of a literary critical approach that emphasizes the nature of the text above everything. It denies the ability of the reader to reconstruct authorial intent and emphasizes only the readers' interpretation of any given text, be that text the back of a matchbox or Leo Tolstoy's *War and Peace*; it doesn't matter. It is what the reader draws out of the text that is important. This is a literary critical approach that, since history is a text-based discipline, you can imagine has severe ramifications for the study of the past. The Post-Modernist historian would deny that we can ever reconstruct the past. We cannot get behind the text that we read about the past. Post-Modernists talk about constructing history, rather than reconstructing it. How do you construct history? You construct history in your own image. You construct history in the image of your own cultural prejudices, gender biases, racial prejudices, or whatever. So, the act of the Post-Modernist historian who is coming to enlighten us is to deconstruct the history and present us with—show us all our foibles and failings—present a history of the past that really suits the position of the teller of the story. I don't intend to adopt a Post-Modernist or Positivist approach in this course. I extend my apologies to Positivists and Post-Modernists who might be watching or listening.

I intend instead to adopt broadly the New Historical approach. I believe that comparative data and the insights of the social sciences can be very helpful when we look at the societal aspects of our subject. For the political and military spheres, we have a lot of ancient evidence about those subjects, so I can adopt a broadly positivist approach there. The Post-Modernist view, I am afraid, will not be one that is expounded in this course. Just to let you know that the outline I have given you here is really something of a simplification, I can quote you from the preface of a book written as recently as 1979, a major book entitled *The Emperor in the Roman World*, a massive study by a man who is now probably the leading Roman historian of his generation, Fergus Miller, sitting at Oxford. Just to show you that Positivism and New History and Post-Modernism all coexist simultaneously; they are foundations for debate among scholars. The issue of the approach to the ancient evidence itself is a focus of debate. As recently as 1979, Fergus Miller in the preface to his study of the emperor in the Roman world could write:

> "In preparing the work, I have rigidly avoided reading sociological works on kingship and related topics, or studies of monarchic institutions on societies other than those of Greece and Rome. I am purposely conscious that this will have involved considerable losses of percipients, and an awareness of whole ranges of questions that I could have asked. Nonetheless, I am confident that the loss in the opposite case would have been greater. For, to have come to the subject with an array of concepts derived from the study of other societies would merely have made even more unobtainable the proper objective of a historian."

To subordinate himself to the evidence and to the conceptual world of the society of the past, that is a positivist. That is at least a summary of the positivistic view. The purpose of the historian is to subordinate himself to the evidence.

So much for the approach to the evidence, what is the ancient material like? Broadly speaking it falls into two classes, archaeological and written evidence. Archaeological evidence is defined as any and all physical material from the ancient past. So, you can imagine that it encompasses a wide array of evidence. I have classified it into macro- and micro-evidence. Macro-evidence, forms of evidence would be entire cities. We have innumerable cities from the ancient world, the most famous probably being Pompeii, buried by Vesuvius in A.D. 79, buried under mounds of volcanic ash and Herculaneum, also buried by Vesuvius on the same day, but buried under volcanic mud. There are cities as well spread all over the Roman Empire. We find cities buried in the sand of Tunisia and Syria, or the remnants of forts, cities and towns in northern England. So, the macro-evidence would embrace cities and buildings and large artifacts that have been identified through archaeological investigation. Not all of it was conducted, by the way, in the best scientific way.

I also believe that the macro-evidence would include some dramatic evidence, for instance bodies. We get bodies from graves and burials. Burials are one of the chief sources of archaeological evidence. Then, from the Vesuvian cities comes incredibly dramatic evidence of people who were killed in the disaster that overtook these places on the 24th of August, A.D. 79. The excavators, when they were digging through the ash would occasionally encounter cavities in the ash, and to find out what was in there, they rather cleverly poured plaster of Paris into the cavity, let it set and excavated around. All kinds of perishable objects, wood, chairs, doors, pieces of furniture would show up, and occasionally, they would find Pompeians and Romans who had perished in the disaster. Some of those finds are extremely dramatic. So, really the macro-evidence is the body of evidence that comes from the ancient world that is large and readily identifiable and in certain cases can be particularly dramatic as from the towns in and around Pompeii and Herculaneum.

The micro-evidence offers us something of a different form which would be all the bits and pieces that show up in and around the macro-evidence as you are excavating it. It is extremely valuable. Undoubtedly the chief form of evidence here would be pottery. Pottery is fired clay. It is imperishable. It can be smashed into small fragments, but it does not biodegrade, so it survives in the soil for as long as it is in there. Vast quantities of pottery have come up from the ancient world; they have been subjected to extremely close analysis and study and can tell us an awful lot about the ancient economy, trade routes and so forth. If you go back into the very ancient past, we also get analysis of pottery stockpiles and decoration to help identify one culture from the other. So, pottery is one of the chief forms of micro-evidence finds, if you like to think of them that way, that crop up from archaeological remains. We also get textiles and bones. The bones of animals can tell you what sort of herds they had. On very rare occasions we find textiles, because textiles degrade rapidly. Only in extremely dry or damp conditions do textiles survive. Now, with the extremely profitable marriage of science and archaeology, we can use microscopes to identify things like pollen, which can also tell you what the grass was like, what particular genus of grass was growing beside the Roman villa, for instance, at this or that time. The micro-evidence can really be micro. It can be down to the cellular level when you use electron microscopes.

Archaeological excavation is an extremely valuable tool. I must stress though that it is essentially a destructive process. When you excavate a site, you are, for all intents and purposes, destroying it. You can't go back and do it again. Once you have excavated the site, you have disrupted the strata of the site, and it can't be done again. So, excavation these days is conducted very carefully, and the key job for all archaeologists is to publish their findings. Without the publication of their findings, all that data dies with them, and no one ever knows what they found there. Archaeological evidence is incredibly useful for identifying what the physical environment of the ancient world was like, but its chief drawback is that it is mute. It's only valuable when it is interpreted. A pot is a pot is a pot. When it is interpreted, when it is analyzed and put together with other evidence to construct trading patterns, then it tells us something about the ancient past. The evidence itself is mute, and as I like to say, if you excavate a Roman villa, that is well and good. We can look at the ground plan of the villa, identify the bathing rooms, the dining rooms, and sleeping cubicles and so forth. What we can't tell is what were the hopes and dreams of the people who lived in the villa. What did they believe? How did they look at the world? What stories did they tell their children at night? We can't tell any of that from the archaeological evidence. For that sort of information you have to go to the written evidence.

Luckily, in the study of ancient Rome, we have a large body, albeit circumscribed, a large body of written evidence. As I said in the first lecture, it is still not as large as it once was. But it is still a fairly significant amount. Written evidence can be subdivided broadly into two categories, ancient literature and inscriptions, or what is termed epigraphic material. Ancient literature is that body of data that has survived over the centuries from the end of antiquity to the modern era, usually by being copied by monks, overwhelmingly, in the Middle Ages. It comprises a large, vast array of genres. We have all kinds of poetry, epic, elegy, love poetry, pastoral poetry. We have all kinds of letters, correspondence between people, speeches, works written by the ancients about Roman history. Hence, we have history written by the ancients as well, which are of primary importance for our interests in this course, but you also have a wide variety of other styles—plays, genres, of literature. All of that gives us insight when it is interpreted properly. It gives us insight into the lives of the ancients, into how they viewed the world, so it is invaluable as a supplement to the archaeological evidence. When one uses written and archaeological evidence together, the results can be spectacular.

On the other hand, the material has survived in copy form. Often, our very earliest texts of this or that author will date only to the 13th, 14th or even 15th centuries. As a result, to a certain degree, it is not pure chance that has allowed these manuscripts to survive. It is because they have been selected. To a certain degree, they have been selected by the people who copied them. Something of value was seen in them, and so it was worth the laborious job of copying out these ancient manuscripts and passing them down from generation to generation. To a certain degree that selected body of text, not entirely, the vicissitudes of chance still apply, but to a certain degree, it is still a selected body of data.

When we turn to the other main body of written evidence for the ancient world, inscriptions, this is not the case. Inscriptions speak to us directly from the ancient past. Inscriptions are a class of data that are invaluable for looking at the ancient world. They are carved on stone, metal or bone, or they are written on proto-paper called papyrus. Sometimes they are written on coins, as we will see, at the end of this lecture. They contain an enormous variety of written information in themselves. If you were to think, what is the most common kind of inscription that exists in the modern world? It is the epitaph. "Here lies Uncle Joe, RIP." The same is true for the inscriptions from the ancient world, from the Latin-speaking world. Epitaphs comprise perhaps 70 percent, maybe 80 percent of our epigraphic data from the Roman past. Unlike rather terse epitaphs of the modern age, they can be extremely fulsome and give us lots of information about the person writing them, especially if that person has taken part in public life. Usually, all the offices that person had would be listed. Again, you can imagine, when collated, assembled and studied quantitatively, they can prove extremely useful.

Besides epitaphs, there are all kinds of other inscriptions the ancients put up. There are treaties. They would put up laws, tables of laws pertaining to this or that town. They would put up commemorative inscriptions. "X built this bathhouse." "Y restored this portico." They would put up inscriptions that accompanied honorary statues of important people. "Here is this statue of this great guy from a local fealty." Why? Well, because he gave all this money for a public banquet or whatever. So, you have honorary and commemorative inscriptions of all sorts. You also have interesting texts that are letters, letters from important people to backward, nowhere-type places. If the emperor takes notice of your town for whatever reason, that is just the sort of thing that you commission to have carved on stone and stuck in the forum of your town. "Look, the emperor has taken notice of our little town." So, we can get imperial documents of all sorts as well carved on stone.

Inscriptions as well extend to the more varied and less formal form. In extraordinary circumstances, we can have inscriptions that are painted on walls, inscriptions that are actually pieces of graffiti. There are some I could quote, but they are actually unquotable, because, just like modern bathroom graffiti, they aren't the subtlest of messages. Also, from Pompeii, there is a very interesting body of data that we would not have otherwise surmised existed are local election notices. They are the equivalent of our election posters, painted on the walls outside houses. "Vote for this guy for the local mayor-ship." What I find a very amusing one, a real sign of how these can tell you the Romans were people too, you have anti-election notices. The thieves of Pompeii recommend that you vote for this guy, because we know him to be efficient at his job. Unlike the literary material, inscriptions speak to us directly from the past. They have not been selected or copied; they turn up often in archaeological finds. Sometimes they have been reused; they have been built into later walls. Sometimes they were reused even in the ancient past. If a later culture came through and wanted to build a fort, and there was a Roman town nearby, why go quarry all the stone? Just take the Roman town down, and often some of those stones have been inscribed. You will go along and find an inscription built into a medieval wall or into a medieval church or cathedral. It is very striking evidence. That is, it is striking for the continuity between the ancient and medieval world. Inscriptions can be found in all sorts of contexts, not just dug up in scientific archaeological excavation.

The ancient written evidence does have its limitations. In the case of literature, it is all written by men who lived mostly in Rome. Think of the size of the empire. It is all written by men who came from a certain class. No male slaves wrote anything that we have that has survived, and very few women. What is more, it is mostly written between the period 200 B.C. and A.D. 200. Most Roman literature falls within that chronological bracket. So, it is a very focused body of material that addresses the interest of upper class males living in Rome in this four hundred year period. Inscriptions likewise are largely formulaic. While epitaphs, laws and election notices can all be very informative, they are nonetheless a certain style or class of material. They tend to use the same sort of language again and again. An honorary inscription commemorating the erection of a building will have the same sort of formulae again and again, whether it was found in Syria, Scotland, France or Germany. You have the same sort of data. It is not like you are going to find an inscription that is the life story of the Emperor Claudius carved on stone. That is not what is going to turn up. So again, it is limited. It is valuable, but it is limited.

I want to close with two odd types of ancient evidence in a class by themselves. That would be coins and papyrus. Coins, especially Roman imperial coins are the model for our modern coins. They had on one side the head of the ruler, usually with an inscription around the side of the head saying what a great guy he was and identifying him in one of his titles. So, they can be dated very precisely. On the other side, on the side opposite the head, they would often have propaganda messages—usually saying what a wonderful place the Roman Empire is to live in and what a good job Emperor X is doing of ruling it. So, coins are sort of quasi-archaeological, quasi-written material at once. They can be studied as archaeological artifacts in and of themselves, or they can be read as texts.

Papyrus is an even odder form of data that derive from extremely dry or extremely wet conditions. It is the form of ancient paper, written in ink. Probably the most famous collection of papyri are the Dead Sea Scrolls from the ancient past, a very unique find, but again, a very rare form of evidence and demanding a high degree of specialized skill in reading them.

So, that is the value and the body of ancient material, wide-ranging, broad, but nonetheless limited and always open to varying interpretation.

Lecture Three
Pre-Roman Italy and the Etruscans

Scope:

In this lecture we briefly survey the geography of ancient Italy and the political and cultural situation that obtained there in the pre-Roman period. The peninsula was mostly inhabited by tribal peoples speaking a variety of Italic languages. The two major exceptions to this pattern of tribal settlement were the Greek colonizers in south Italy and Sicily and the Etruscans in the region immediately north of Rome. We end the lecture by examining in outline the main characteristics of Etruscan civilization.

Outline

I. The geography of the Italian peninsula offered many benefits to its inhabitants.

    A. The peninsula is well-watered and well-endowed with natural resources.

        1. The Alps in the north and the Apennine range that runs down the center of Italy provide springs, streams, and rivers more than sufficient to supply the inhabitants.

        2. The largest rivers in Italy, and the ones with which we shall be mostly concerned, are the Po and Arno Rivers in the north, and the Tiber in central Italy.

        3. The mountainous nature of the country guaranteed an abundance of wood and ores for the ancient Italians, and pasture for sheep and goats.

    B. The plains are fertile.

        1. The three main plains in Italy are the Po River valley in the north, the plain of Latium around Rome, and Campania around Naples.

        2. Campania, in particular, with its volcanic soil, pleasant climate, and natural hot springs, was destined to become a popular pleasure spot for the Roman elite.

        3. The plain of Latium, on the north edge of which lay the Tiber River and the site of Rome, is surrounded by the sea to the west and mountains to the east. A range of low hills (the Alban hills) is located in the center of the plain.

4. All of these plains are fertile. By the time of Roman expansion into Italy, all were inhabited by settled people practicing agriculture.

II. With the exception of the Greek colonizers and the Etruscans, pre-Roman Italy was inhabited by non-urbanized tribal peoples.

    A. The tribal cultures of pre-Roman Italy are difficult to study.

        1. Archaeology shows that Italy had human inhabitants as early as the Stone Age.

        2. Literary sources become available only in the fifth century B.C., by which time the immediately pre-Roman tribal cultures of Italy had existed for 500 years or more.

        3. The situation before ca. 400 B.C. is therefore very hard to reconstruct.

    B. Pre-Roman tribal Italy was a quilt of languages and cultures.

        1. Archaeology and linguistics are our main avenues for studying this period. Two archaeological keys are burial styles and pottery.

        2. At least 40 languages and dialects have been determined.

        3. A broad division appears to have existed between settled agriculturists in the plains and their threatening, mountain-dwelling neighbors.

        4. The situation in 400 B.C. was as follows, north to south: the Celtic Gauls had control of the Po Valley, the Etruscans were to their south, then came the Romans and the Latins, the Oscans and Samnites controlled central Italy and parts of Campania, and the Greeks were found in the south.

    C. The Greeks and Etruscans were urbanized cultures.

        1. The Greek colonies in Italy were localized affairs and centered on coastal cities, notably Naples and Tarentum.

        2. The Etruscans, too, were an urbanized people and much influenced by the Greeks (i.e., "Hellenized").

III. The Etruscans.

    A. The origins of the Etruscans are unclear.

        1. No Etruscan literature survives; they are studied through archaeology, later Roman tales about them, mentions in Greek sources, and surviving inscriptions in their ill-understood language.

2. They may have been migrants from the eastern Mediterranean.
3. More likely, they were a native Italian culture (called "Villanovan") that became urbanized c. 800–700 B.C., perhaps through contact with the Greeks.

B. They were not a politically unified people.
1. The Etruscans were very influential in Italy but not unified.
2. They had a League of Twelve Cities, which often warred with each other.
3. They were united by language and religion, and the Cities could occasionally work in concert.
4. Originally ruled by kings, many Etruscan cities became oligarchies, ruled by councils of leading families.

C. The nature of Etruscan "control" in Italy is unclear.
1. Earlier scholars imagined a sort of "Etruscan Empire" in Italy, stretching from the Po Valley to Campania. This empire collapsed in the fifth and fourth centuries B.C. in the face of resistance from the Greeks in the south and incursions of Gauls in the north.
2. More recently, it has been proposed that there was a looser sphere of Etruscan influence, predominantly on the cultural plane; there was no "Etruscan Empire."
3. This debate affects how historians read the early history of Rome, particularly the question of "Etruscan Rome" under the last kings.

D. The Etruscans were absorbed by the Romans, but they greatly influenced Roman culture.
1. The main areas of Etruscan influence on the Romans were in religion and statecraft, but also in architecture.
2. From the late third century B.C. onwards, the Etruscans were thoroughly absorbed into the Roman state, and by the age of the emperors they had ceased to exist as a distinct cultural group.

Essential Reading:

T. J. Cornell, *The Beginnings of Rome*, chapters 1–2.

Supplemental Reading:

R. M. Ogilvie, *Early Rome and the Etruscans*, esp. chapters 1–3.

G. Barker, *The Etruscans*.

Questions to Consider:

1. How reliable are modern scholars' reconstructions of the situation in pre-Roman Italy? On what evidence are they based, and how is that evidence deployed by modern scholars?

2. Which of the modern views of the nature of Etruscan in Italy do you favor? Why?

Lecture Three—Transcript
Pre-Roman Italy and the Etruscans

Welcome to the third lecture in The History of Ancient Rome. Having surveyed the introductory materials in the first two lectures, it is now time to turn our attention to the ancient world itself. What I intend to do in this lecture is set the situation as it existed in pre-Roman Italy. The Romans were not the first people to inhabit the Italian peninsula. They were not even the first people to become powerful or influential within the Italian peninsula. It is worth examining what the situation was and what the Romans felt as they emerged as a major power in the region in the fourth and third centuries B.C. I will begin by looking at the overall geography of the Italian peninsula and how it benefited the ancient inhabitants there. Then we will examine, in sequence, the non-urbanized tribal cultures of pre-Roman Italy, the Greek colonists in the southern part of Italy and in Sicily, (We will treat them rather briefly.) and then we will look at the people who were often erroneously described as mysterious, the Etruscans, who are not really all that mysterious at all, as we will see.

First, we will look at the geography of the Italian peninsula as a whole. Italy is very well watered because of its mountainous nature. In the north are the towering Alpine ranges, which are perennially snowbound and so offer plenty of rivers and streams to the northern part of the peninsula. Down the spine of Italy (if you want to think of it as a boot the way I was told; think of Italy as the boot kicking Sicily, which I think is metaphorically really quite accurate) are the Apennine mountains. They are not as high as the Alps and not permanently snowbound, but they do offer, especially in the wintertime, an abundance of water, streams and springs to feed the inhabitants. The largest rivers in Italy (at least the ones that we are going to be the most focused on) are three: the Po River in the north which runs from east to west, sort of from the land over toward Venice, the Arno River in north-central Italy, which was one of the borders of the ancient Etruscan homeland, and then in central Italy the Tiber River, which is the river on which Rome was founded. The mountainous nature of Italy also offered the people plenty of wood and pastureland for sheep and goats, which were raised in great profusion as archaeology makes clear, and still are to this day.

Aside from the mountains, there are coastal plain areas in Italy, and three of those are worth looking at. The first one isn't actually coastal, it is the Po Valley, the river valley of that major river in the north of Italy, which offers a very wide expanse, the widest expanse in the country, of fertile, arable land. Also, we will be looking at the plain of Latium, modern-day Lazio, which is immediately to the south of the settlement of Rome. The Latins, as we will see, were to receive the close attention of the Romans for several centuries before the rest of the Italians and ultimately the rest of the inhabitants of the Mediterranean did. South of Latium around the area of Naples is the plain of Campania. Campania is extremely fertile because it has Mount Vesuvius located in it. Mount Vesuvius is an active volcano and erupted most spectacularly in recent memory in 1879 burying the cities of Pompeii and Herculaneum, leaving us with a great archaeological treasure trove. Also, it offers the Plain of Campania an agricultural treasure trove of volcanic minerals that make the place especially fertile and, because the slopes of the mountain, was a very popular place for wine growing in ancient times. As an aside, I will presage some later talk about public leisure by saying that Campania became the equivalent of the Roman aristocracy's Florida. This is where they went to holiday and relax. It is a beautiful environment. There is a saying, "See the Bay of Naples and die." It is a great physical setting, but also there are naturally hot springs and so forth there, and very quickly the plane of Campania and the towns around it became holiday resorts for the Roman well-to-do.

As to Latium itself, it is bordered on its northern edges as I have said by the River Tiber, on its western side by the Mediterranean Sea and on its east and south by mountains. In the center of the Plain of Latium, down the Alban Hills are a low-laying range of hills which were to be a religious focal point for the people, the early inhabitants of Latium, the Latins. By the time of Roman expansion in Italy, all these plains and the other ones I haven't mentioned, the low lands of Italy, were well worked by agriculturists. In the mountains tended to reside more pastoral people (more of that later on), but this was a well-settled region by the time the Romans emerged as a power in the area of Italy.

What about the people themselves? With the exception of the Greek colonizers in the south and the Etruscans in ancient Etruria, modern Tuscany, the Italian peninsula was occupied by non-urbanized, tribal peoples. That means these peoples did not have large cities. They tended to live in villages in loose tribal arrangements led by chieftains (or clans). They often would have specific sites they shared for religious purposes, which offered a focal point for their cultures, but they were living what would be termed by archaeologists as an Iron Age lifestyle—a tribal, non-urbanized lifestyle. Archaeology is clear that the first inhabitants of Italy went back to the Stone Age. The period before about 400 B.C. is very difficult to reconstruct. We have fragmentary references by Greeks to the situation in Italy prior to 400 B.C., but they are extremely sketchy and lain over with legends and myth which makes it very difficult for the historian trying to reconstruct the situation in the era before 400 B.C.

Our two main avenues into the prehistoric period of Italy are archaeology and linguistics. Archaeology as we have seen before is a very valuable tool for the ancient historian churning up an enormous variety of ancient evidence, ancient artifacts which can be studied. Then there is the prehistoric period, that means the period before we have any kind of extant or consistent literary or written evidence whatsoever, archaeology is really all we have to work on. As we have already seen, from looking at archaeology, everything then depends on the interpretation of the data. It is safe to say that archaeology offers us two ways of examining and trying to make sense of the cultural patterns of pre-Roman Italy. One is examination of burial styles, whether the people inhumed their dead (buried them whole) or whether they cremated them. Often cultures can be determined by whether or not they used cremation of inhumation. The other main avenue is pottery styles. Types of pottery, types of pots and decorative techniques on those pots are also used in combination with burial styles and settlement patterns to try to deduce the different classes of people who occupied early Italy. This course is not about early Italy, so I am not going to go into tremendous detail about the various types of cultures that have been located there. Suffice it to say that now a reasonably good picture of the situation in prehistoric Italy can be reconstructed. We see people in there from the Stone Age that continue into the Bronze Age and around 1000 B.C., there is a tremendous growth in population of the pre-Roman people of Italy. They start to become more profuse; their settlements become more common, and their burials become more common because there are more people to bury.

What about linguistic evidence? Linguistic evidence is also very useful. So far at least 40 languages have been identified that were spoken in pre-Roman Italy—40 languages or dialects of languages might be more accurate, which is quite a lot. These dialects are known to us from often fragmentary inscriptions that have been found inscribed on stone or pieces of pottery. They are in fossils that have been left over in later authors who quote ancient formulae that seem to incorporate these ancient languages. What is the historical significance of the linguistic evidence? What does the plethora of languages and their various classifications tell us about the historical processes that determined the population pattern of pre-Roman Italy? That is a much more difficult question to answer. Are we talking about language groups supplanting other language groups because of invasion, because of conquest, or because of trade, emulation, migration, and acculturation? What is going on? What is the historical process behind the quilt of pre-Roman Italic languages? That is a matter for debate, and we will leave that to the experts in the field. I just want to draw your attention to it.

As far as we can tell, the broad division between the peoples of pre-Roman Italy was that of agriculturalists in the low land and often very warlike pastoralist people living in the hills or foothills of the mountains that are so common across the peninsula. Sometime around 600 B.C., a major shift took place in the population of Italy in the north. Starting at about this time, people from across the Alps began to infiltrate into the northern part of Italy. These people were Celts, what the Romans called "Gauls," Gallic Celtic people who were in Northern Europe a very dominant Iron Age culture. The Celts seem to have arisen in the area of Austria originally, spread westward to eventually occupy most of France and parts of Germany, Spain and eventually they moved up into the British Isles where they founded the civilization which has given us such wonderful scholars of ancient Rome.

Starting around 600 B.C., they also began to cross the Alps. This would have been some feat. Crossing the Alps without anything but goat tracks to follow must have been quite difficult. What is happening? Are these Celtic invasions? Are these large bodies of armed men coming in and taking over the northern part of Italy, the Po Valley, or are they gradual migrations, filtrations that take place over centuries? It is very hard to tell that from the archaeological evidence, which will tend to conflate the evidence giving you 50 years on either side. 50 years is a long time. It is almost two generations of people. What is going on it very hard to say. We can say that by 500 B.C., the whole of the Po Valley was occupied by Gallic Celts. In fact, the Romans called it Gallia Cisalpina, which means "Gaul, this side of the Alps." They classified it as part of the land of the Gauls, and it was not until much later that it became classified as part of Italy. Italia started south of Gallia Cisalpina. The whole northern plane was originally considered by the Romans as not a part of Italy.

In the picture of pre-Roman Italy, we have the Celtic Gauls in the north. Then we have the various Italic tribal cultures, chief among them in central Italy, the Oscans and the Samnites (We will be hearing more about the Samnites occupying the area to the south and east of Latium.) In the south of Italy we also have invaders called Greeks. They were not quite invaders; they were foreign settlers, people from abroad. What are the Greeks doing in Italy? Those of you who know Greek history will be well familiar with the period of Greek colonization that started around 800 B.C. and continued on to about 600 B.C. The intense period of colonization stretched from 800 B.C. to 700 B.C.—the very intense spread of Greeks and their culture across the Mediterranean world. They went east and west. They went up into the Black Sea and the southern extent of Russia, and they also came westward as far as Italy. In fact, some of the earliest colonization from Greece took place in Italy. By the time that the Romans began to emerge as a force to be reckoned with in Italy, the Greeks were well established in the southern part of Italy and in Sicily. But, a word on Greek colonies and Greek colonization: Greek colonies were not part of any organized, centralized Greek empire or Greek state. They were not instruments of *imperium*. They were instead each city-states, each independent of the other, each with its own laws and governing bodies, foreign policy, coinage, army and so forth. So, these Greek colonies cannot be seen as part of a concerted attempt by Greece to take over Italy or anything like that. They are merely a pattern of settlement in the southern part of Italy that would have been well established by the time the Romans emerged on the scene. The Greek colonies that we would be talking about most commonly are: Naples, Neapolis (the New City), which was founded on the coast of Campania on the mainland, Tarentum, which is down south and east of the southern shore of Sicily (that was to be a major player in Roman history) and finally, possibly the most powerful Greek city-state anywhere in the Greek world, Syracuse on Sicily. This was a very powerful state and one to be reckoned with and one the Romans saw fit to ally themselves with before they attempted to take the place over and conquer it.

The Greeks are different from the people that we have looked at. These are urbanized, highly sophisticated people. Greek culture is a very influential culture, and the process that describes the adoption of Greek ways of doing things, or Greek thought for example, is Hellenization, from the Greek word "Hellas," which is how they describe themselves, the Hellenes. Hellenization is the process of people adopting Greek manners. Wherever the Greeks went, people who neighbored them tended to get Hellenized. It tends to be that the simpler culture will emulate the more sophisticated culture. That seems to be general anthropological principle. The Greeks were about as sophisticated as the Mediterranean could get at that time. So, the influence of the Greeks should not be underestimated. It seems that some time around the arrival of the Greeks in south Italy and Sicily, peoples to the north of Rome became very heavily Hellenized, pre-Roman peoples called Villanovans (It is a strange name, but it is the name of the site where the pottery style that defined the culture was found) seem to have risen up to civilization and become known to us as the Etruscans. It is on the Etruscans that I will focus the last part of this lecture.

The Etruscans are often described as mysterious. In popular culture, they are still presented as being somehow mysterious. This view is somewhat understandable, but it is not entirely correct. We have nothing from the Etruscans themselves in terms of long literary treatments of their own history or culture like we do for the Greeks and the Romans. We have details of outsiders about them. We have details of the Romans about them. We have details of the Greeks about them. We have archaeological evidence which is invaluable. We also have inscriptions in the Etruscan language. You think, if we have inscriptions, don't we have material from the Etruscans? Yes, we do but the problem is we can't read it. It was written in Greek letters. So, we can read what the words say, we just don't know what they mean. As a result, bits and pieces of Etruscan inscriptions can be understood, but for the most part we can't use the material to reconstruct a history of the Etruscans in tremendous detail the way we can for the Greeks or the Romans. On the other hand, investigation into the Etruscan world, in the last 50 years especially, has revealed an awful lot to us about them that now makes it possible to say that they are really not all that mysterious. There are still questions about the Etruscans, their origins (that we are going to look at) and the nature of their control and their influence in Italy. These are certainly valid historical questions. But, what Etruscan society was like broadly speaking, that we can now safely say we can present in a reasonably clear way.

The ancient view of the Etruscans was that they were immigrants from the eastern Mediterranean. This would certainly explain why their language was so odd since it bears no resemblance to any of the neighboring Italic languages of the ancient peoples bordering the Etruscan lands. Naturally enough, one can say if their language is so odd, maybe they brought it with them from elsewhere. For the longest time it was considered to be the case that the Greeks and the Romans were right. The Etruscans were foreigners who had migrated from the eastern half of the Mediterranean. Precisely where is unclear, but somewhere in the east wherever that is, and they had settled for some reason in the area of ancient Etruria, which is the area immediately north of Rome bordered by the Tiber River on the south, the Arno River on the north, by the Apennine Mountains on the east and the sea on the west. More recently, a lot of archaeological work has revealed that in all likelihood the Etruscans are native Italian peoples called Villanovans, who raised themselves up to urbanize civilization probably/possibly under influence from the Greeks. The archaeological evidence shows that under all the Etruscan sites, there is a Villanovan site. There is no sign of any discontinuity of settlements, invasion, burning, or anything that might suggest that the Etruscans came into a situation aggressively, as was the old view of the origins of the Etruscans. So, I think we can say relatively safely that on the best available current evidence the Etruscans are a native Italian, urbanized culture, but under strong Greek influence. That is always important to remember about them.

The Etruscans were not a unified people politically. They had city-states. We hear of a league of twelve cities. It seems there were mutually antagonistic members of this league who often warred with each other but could act in concerted efforts if threatened or if it was to their advantage. They do seem to have come together for religious purposes. In other words, this is a very common feature of leagues, especially in Greece where often antagonistic, warring city-states can come together to celebrate festivals—religious festivals or aesthetic festivals—together. That is an interesting parallel with the Greeks among the Etruscan cities. The cities themselves appear to have originally been ruled by kings. Again, like the Greeks, by the time that the Romans began to encounter them seriously, many of those cities had undergone revolutions. The kings had been overthrown and they were ruled by what are termed oligarchies. (There is a technical term to impress people at Thanksgiving dinner. "That's a nice oligarchy you have there.") An oligarchy is a rule of a few, a handful, of people, determined either by birth or by wealth or some other criterion that demarcates the ruling class from the non-ruling class.

There is no doubt that the Etruscans exercised a tremendous influence over central Italy. Debate has recently been rekindled as to the nature of that influence. This is a good example of the sorts of interpretive issues that pervade ancient history that we talked about in the introductory materials. This is an important question. What was the nature of the Etruscan control in Italy? It is a very basic question. It is one that we should be able to answer reasonably, but it turns out to be very difficult. The perceived view—the view that was very common and is still very common—is that the Etruscans exercised strong political control over Italy from the Po Valley south to Campania. They exercised this primarily on the western seaboard of Italy, but they also crossed the Apennines and exercised some control in the area of modern day Umbria. This was, if you want to think of it this way, an empire or kingdom of the Etruscans. If you think about the geography that we just looked at, Rome and the Latins will be in the middle of that empire. At some stage, by the logic of this reconstruction, the Romans must have been ruled by the Etruscans. People have gone, and they have found strong evidence that the Romans were at one stage under the thumb of their northern neighbors. There is talk of an Etruscan period in Roman history. This is a very common view and it has a lot of supporting evidence in its favor.

Recently, a very stimulating book was published by Tim Cornell in England called *The Beginnings of Rome*. Tim Cornell challenges this view of Etruscan domination in Italy. He points out inconsistencies in the pattern of Etruscan evidence across the so-called Empire. He says, for instance, if you look at the density of inscriptions we have lots of Etruscan inscriptions pertaining to important people. (One didn't carve an inscription for a nobody. One carved for an important person.) We have lots of those inscriptions in Etruria itself, north of Rome, not very many in Latium, and then a lot in Campania. Why do we have an Etruscan Empire with a big hole in the middle? Why are there so many Etruscans north and south of Latium but not in Latium itself? He also draws parallels with other archaic cultures looking at the nature of the upper classes in these archaic cultures, and how they can move around freely among each other, across these state boundaries. There is an aristocratic ethos among these early cultures, and this does not fit with the notion of an Etruscan dominance. His picture of the nature of Etruscan control in central Italy is of a sphere of influence. Many of the pieces of evidence that you find for the early Etruscan Empire or the Etruscan Empire in Italy are actually evidence of cultural influence. That can't be denied. So, in Etruria, you have plenty of Etruscans, and they move south passing by Latium (maybe going by the sea) into Campania, which is extremely pleasant as I have mentioned before. You find plenty of Etruscans down there, but not too many in the area of Latium itself which was densely populated and would be a very difficult place to conquer -- as the Romans found out. It was very difficult to move into militarily and take over. So, it was simply bypassed by the Etruscans.

What we are talking about then is not so much an Etruscan empire or an extended Etruscan kingdom in control of central Italy, but rather, a sphere of influence—a sphere of cultural and undoubtedly political influence as well. It was not a centralized state or empire. Whether or not Tim Cornell's view will ever be accepted in full is a matter for scholars to figure out over the next few years. Initial reactions have been mixed. Some people are horrified to see the notion of Etruscan Rome being so hastily dismissed, and the issue will no doubt be hotly debated by students of early Rome and of the Etruscans for years to come. It is interesting that there is such a debate and fully illustrative of what we talked about in the introductory classes of this course, the sort of things that people argue about in ancient history.

The Etruscans were very thoroughly absorbed by the Romans. This is one of the reasons they were initially considered to be so mysterious. Drawing the line between Etruscan and Roman in so many fields has proven to be very difficult. The Romans tended to look at their own culture and say "That is an odd feature of the way we do things? Where did that come from? The Etruscans gave us that, and we don't know if we can trust that statement or not." The Romans seem to have thrown it out as having come from the

Etruscans. "That is why we have a temple shaped like that. That is why we look at birds to try to divine the nature of the gods' intent." That is a very strange thing to do isn't it? To go out and look at birds feeding or birds flying, (it is called auguring) and that way you are able to tell something about the gods' disposition toward this or that endeavor that you are planning to take part in. This is something the Romans say came from the Etruscans. In fact, the evidence of tomb paintings from archaeological sites would suggest that this is not incorrect. It seems that the Etruscans were keen on this issue of divination, trying to divine closely the attitude of the gods toward human enterprises.

The Romans were also greatly influenced by the Etruscans in issues of statecraft, especially the symbols of power. We will see those symbols of power when we look at the Roman Republic. Suffice it to say now that many of those symbols (for instance the *fasces*, the rods and axes of office that accompanied Roman magistrates) were derived from the Etruscans. We will see other influences on the Roman polity, at least under symbols of power, from the Etruscan sources.

Pre-Roman Italy then is a quilt of cultures with a great variety of languages, with some foreigners, Greeks in the south, Celts in the north, and the whole place while not waiting for Rome, certainly going to experience Rome in no short order in the centuries to come.

Lecture Four
The Foundation of Rome

Scope:

The two stories of Rome's foundation, which was traditionally dated to 753 B.C., are well known. Both stories, that of Romulus and Remus and that of Aeneas, are outlined and discussed in this lecture. The archaeological evidence, which tells a somewhat different but not incompatible story, is also presented. In conclusion, we examine how the question of Rome's foundation offers an excellent window onto the relative merits of archaeological and written evidence when they are deployed together in pursuit of a specific historical problem.

Outline

I.   Later Romans preserved two tales of the foundation of their city.

    A. The story of Romulus and Remus was probably a local folk legend.

        1. Romulus and Remus escaped death as infants and founded Rome.

        2. The story has characteristic folkloric elements that suggest it is very old and local in origin.

    B. The story of Aeneas derives from a Hellenized source, reflecting Greek legends.

        1. Aeneas, the sole survivor of Troy, wandered the Mediterranean before settling in Italy at Lavinium, where he founded a town.

        2. This legend must derive from a Greek or at least Hellenized source, but it is probably older than many have assumed.

        3. The two stories were united into a single tradition by making Romulus and Remus descendants of Aeneas.

        4. Aeneas founded the Roman people; Romulus and Remus founded the city of Rome.

II. Archaeological evidence suggests that settlement at Rome began as early as 1500 B.C., but it does not offer any evidence that substantially contradicts the ancient legends.

    A. The site of Rome was advantageous.

        1. It overlooked a ford in the Tiber near an island in the stream; it could control north-south traffic between

Etruria and Latium and east-west traffic from the interior to the coast.

2. It was hilly, defensible, and well-watered.
3. Signs of early human habitation (i.e., pottery shards) date to c. 1500 B.C., with the first permanent settlement, as indicated by graves, founded in c. 1000 B.C.

B. Originally, Rome was a series of separate villages; evidence of these settlements has been found.

1. From then, and into the eighth century B.C., Rome developed as a series of small villages on neighboring hilltops.
2. At some stage—dates are impossible to establish—these communities coalesced into a single community and Rome, as an entity, was born.
3. Spectacular finds on the Palatine Hill in Rome in the 1930s revealed postholes for wooden huts that dated to the mid-eighth century, c. 750 B.C.
4. Later Romans maintained a hut on the Palatine that they called "The Hut of Romulus."

III. Archaeology cannot confirm legends.

A. Archaeological evidence needs to be interpreted to make sense.

1. The presence of worship centers embracing Aeneas in Lavinium does not "prove" the Aeneas legend. The worship of Aeneas at Lavinium is likely the result of the fame of the legend, not vice versa.
2. The coincidence of the Palatine huts and the traditional foundation date does not "prove" the Romulus legend. In fact, the settlement of which the huts are part dates to 1000 B.C.
3. Archaeological evidence is mute; it cannot "prove" legendary evidence but occasionally it can disprove it.
4. The archaeology does suggest an early pattern of settlement at Rome, becoming more complex in the eighth century and coalescing into a single community sometime after that (a process termed synoikism).

B. Therefore, the issue of sources for this early period of Roman history is an important consideration to bear in mind.

Essential Reading:

Livy, *The Early History of Rome*, book 1.

T. J. Cornell, *The Beginnings of Rome*, chapter 3.

Supplemental Reading:

C. J. Smith, *Early Rome and Latium: Economy and Society, c. 1000 to 500 B.C.*

Questions to Consider:

1. Where did the ancient Roman authors get their information concerning the early period of Roman history?

2. In what precise respects do the archaeological and written sources converge or diverge in their reconstruction of Rome's founding?

Lecture Four—Transcript
The Foundation of Rome

Welcome to the fourth lecture in The History of Rome for The Teaching Company. Having established the due cultural shape of pre-Roman Italy, it is now time to embark on the long story of Rome by beginning at the beginning, the foundation of Rome itself. In this lecture I wish to outline the stories that the Romans themselves preserved concerning the foundation of the city, and of their nation. Then we will look at the archaeological evidence for the earliest history of the site at Rome itself and its immediate context. We will end with a brief examination of one of the themes that we have been carrying throughout the early part of this course, the issue of the limits of archaeological evidence as illustrated by this one question. Under what circumstances and when was Rome founded? We have literary evidence. We have legendary evidence from the Romans themselves. We have archaeological evidence. Let's put the two together and see what we can come up with.

Later Romans preserved two tales about the origin of their people and their city. Both are well known to most people. One of them surrounds the twins Romulus and Remus. The other surrounds the Trojan hero Aeneas. I'll deal with each of them in sequence. The story about Romulus and Remus is entertaining, so I am going to tell it. It is preserved in numerous versions by the Romans themselves. It is typical in legendary or mythic tales that there are a variety of versions of them floating around the ancient world. The version I am going to give you is that of Livy (Titus Livius) who is one of our best extant sources for the earliest periods of Roman history. Livy wrote a vast history of Rome in 142 books at the time of the Emperor Augustus. So, we are talking about the period around 30 B.C. onwards. He had been working for 40 years on this project. Of those 142 books, 35 books of Livy's history have survived, including the first five, which deal with the very earliest periods of Roman history. It is an invaluable source, at least for what later Romans thought about the earliest phases of their own history.

What I want to tell you now is Livy's version of the story of Romulus and Remus, but there are variants out there, and you may have heard some details that diverge from what I am going to say. Don't worry, if you have. The story starts in Alba Longa, in the plain of Latium, where the king, Numitor, finds himself deposed by his brother Amulius. The villainous Amulius commences murdering the children of his brother, but spares the niece, Rhea Silvia, making her instead a vestal virgin, a calculated appointment since a vestal virgin by nature cannot have children, and no grandsons of Numitor can arise to avenge his usurpation. Rather embarrassingly, Rhea finds herself pregnant. Naturally, this lay at the feet of a god, none other than Mars, the God of War. Not only does she have a son, she has two, twins, Romulus and Remus by name. Amulius is horrified and imprisons Rhea and orders the boys drowned. I've always wondered why they go for drowning. It is like the James Bond movies where they always insist upon talking at great length while they are trying to kill the good guy, giving him a chance to get away, rather than just killing the children straight out. They have to be drowned. They are placed in a basket, and sent down the river. Lo and behold, the basket doesn't sink. It gets washed up on the shores of the River Tiber, where the children are discovered by a she-wolf and suckled, kept alive, until a shepherd happens by, brings the children home, and raises them to adulthood.

As young men, Romulus and Remus perform all sorts of great deeds. They go around being brigands on brigands for instance. They live a sort of Robin Hood lifestyle, robbing the robbers. Rather than distributing the loot among the poor, they just keep it and distribute it among their friends. Eventually, this sort of behavior draws the attention of the king, and Remus is captured and brought before Amulius as a brigand. Then he is sent over to Numitor, who appears to have been a sort of country squire living in relative obscurity. Exactly why he is sent over there is not made entirely clear. He is sent over there, and then a very important moment happens. Here is Remus standing before Numitor and it becomes clear to everyone that this is no brigand. A brigand doesn't have that stature, that noble profile or that fine character. The shepherd reveals, "I have always suspected that maybe these two children were something special. I found them being suckled by a she-wolf." "How long ago was that?" says Numitor. "This long ago." "My goodness." Everything falls into place and it becomes clear that Romulus and Remus are the sons [sic grandsons] of Numitor. They organize a coup, and depose Amulius, in fact they kill him just for good measure, and reinstall Numitor as the king of Alba Longa. So far the whole story revolves around the internal politics of Alba Longa. Here's where a rather tenuous link comes into play. It suddenly grabs the twins that they feel the urge to go and found a new settlement. So, they truck along to where the basket was washed ashore. It just happens to be below the slopes of a hill called the Palatine, which is in the center of modern Rome, and there they found a settlement. The tale ends in tragedy, because Romulus and Remus quarrel over the new settlement.

The two most common reasons given for the quarrel in the ancient sources are that they quarreled over the naming of the settlement. Romulus wanted it named after himself. Remus wanted it named after himself. Presumably, if Remus had won, we would be talking about the great city of Reme on the Tiber. Romulus won the argument in a fashion that had proven most effective in settling arguments throughout history. He killed his brother. The other source for the argument is that Remus mocked the growing walls of the town by jumping over them and showing how small they were. This irritated Romulus so much that in a fit of rage, he killed his brother. Romulus then stood alone as the founder of this new settlement called Rome and became its first king. There we have the Romulus and Remus story, immortalized in all kinds of famous images including the wonderful Capitoline bronze wolf statue today in Rome in the Capitoline museum. It is an Etruscan statue of the wolf, which really attests to the antiquity of this tale. The statue must date to about 600 B.C., although the two suckling babies that are a feature of the statue were added in the Renaissance period. The idea that a wolf is the image of Rome clearly shows that this is a very ancient tale.

Indeed, folklorists would agree. They would argue that this has all the hallmarks of a classic local indigenous folklore legend of the sort that we find repeated again and again in all sorts of cultures around the globe, not just in the Mediterranean. We have special children— royal children who were denied their birthright. There is an attempt to kill those children by some kind of villainous ruler. The children escape miraculously and end up being raised by animals or people of lowly birth. Eventually, their true character shines through and they come back into the story to seize control of their destinies and undo the wrong that was done them and their families in the past. Such images can be found if we just take the biblical contexts from Moses right through to Jesus himself. After all, Herod attempted to kill this supposed king of the Jews. All these stories, images and motifs are found repeatedly in folk stories from Africa to Polynesia in various degrees. As a result, folklorists and most historians agree that this is the original founding legend of the Romans. This is the story that they originally had, the oldest one, to explain where they came from.

The other legend that the Romans preserved about their past comes from a different source. It focuses on the Trojan War. Those of you familiar with Greek culture will be aware that the Trojan War is one of those formative events in the Greek communal mentality. It is the focus of the two great national epics of the Greeks *The Iliad* and *The Odyssey*. It is the source of many of their values. It is the source of some of the great stories from Greek legends: Helen of Troy, the enormous expedition to Troy, Achilles, and so forth—great dueling heroes of the past fighting for honor and country. This is very much a Greek story, and the other Roman foundation legend derives from this source. According to this legend, Aeneas, the last survivor of Troy, following the destruction of the city when it was captured by Greece through subterfuge, flees his burning city, carrying his father on his shoulders, leading his son by his hand, and takes off in a boat, sails across the Mediterranean, undergoing all sorts of wonderful adventures before settling on the coast of Latium and founding this city of Lavitium on the coast of the Plain of Latium in Italy. He also fights various local kings and makes alliances with some kings. The whole legend gets elaborated into an epic story that is most famously commemorated in the Roman national epic poem *The Aeneid* (i.e. the poem about Aeneas,) which is a fine read if you ever get a chance to read it.

This is clearly a Greek legend. This is clearly a Roman origin story that is attempting to tie in with Greek culture. For the longest time it was believed it could only have come into popular appeal among the Romans when they were really trying to emulate Greek culture, probably in the third and second centuries B.C. As we have seen, the Greeks have been present in Italy from at least 800 B.C. The Romans, who were familiar with the Etruscans (they were neighbors of theirs) would have been well familiar with Greek culture long before the third and second centuries B.C. In all likelihood, this story of Aeneas goes back also to the distant past of the Romans, probably not as far as the Romulus and Remus legend, but certainly not as recently as the third and second centuries B.C. Recent archaeological discoveries at the site of Lavinium, the town founded by Aeneas, would suggest that Aeneas was being worshipped there as a god as early as the fourth century B.C. It certainly seems to be the case that this legend is older than many have so far assumed.

There was a problem. "How do we unite these two stories?" Some people had the vague notion that Romulus and Remus were the grandsons of Aeneas, for instance. There is a problem there, because the Romans had already probably arbitrarily decided that the date for the foundation of Rome was 753 B.C. The Trojan War had taken place around 1200 B.C. Unless Romulus and Remus or Aeneas were exceptionally long-lived, they could not be the grandsons, or in the grandfather/grandson type relationship. The solution was reached at some stage, (we are not quite clear when, but certainly by Livy's day) by making the relationship between Aeneas and Romulus more distant. Aeneas founds Lavinium; his son Ascanius (also known as Iulus) founds Alba Longa. Out of the kings of Alba Longa, as we have seen from the Romulus and Remus legend, emerge Romulus and Remus. We have a nice united cycle now of stories of our origins. As a result, they are very cleverly united into a single saga. In a nutshell, then, in the ancient view, Aeneas founded the Roman people. Romulus founded the city that the Roman people were to flourish in.

These are great tales, and very entertaining. How historical are they? Well, that is the $6000 question. Archaeological evidence suggests a somewhat different picture from the origins of Rome. The site of Rome itself is very advantageous. It is located on a series of hills and spurs of hills overlooking a natural ford in the River Tiber where there is an island. It is the only island in the stream of the Tiber, I believe, for its length, close to the sea. So it is a natural place to ford the river. The evidence would suggest that this spot, being very easily defensible, allowing the people who occupied it to control traffic that goes across the river in the north-south axis, and to control traffic that goes inland, upstream, or down from the inland regions toward the sea. This is going to give the people who occupy this site a strong advantage over their neighbors. As a result, it is an attractive place to settle.

It seems that the first signs of human settlement from the archaeological evidence date to about 1500 B.C. They are not signs of permanent settlement but of human presence. There are some burials and some pottery shards and so forth. It is not until about 1000 B.C. that the first signs of permanent settlement show up. Sorry, this is when the burials show up, at about 1000 B.C. The previous evidence was just pottery shards which could have gotten there any way. They could have got there by ships or boats that crashed and people got out and dropped their pots and broke them. It could be the temporary staging post in the river or something like that. The first permanent evidence, which is evidence by burials that indicate people saying we are going to claim this land as our own and bury our ancestors here, that dates to about 1000 B.C.

It seems to summarize the archaeological evidence. It seems to be that originally the settlements on the hills were independent villages. The nature of these villages, who the people were who occupied them, their interrelationships among each other and their relationships with their neighbors are all things that we cannot reconstruct from the archaeological evidence. It does seem that each settlement had its own defensive perimeter and was very much its own place. At some stage, at some early stage (dates now are really impossible) separately, these villages coalesced into a single community. This is the process that we have parallels for in Greek history. It is called by the rather odd sounding term *synoikism*, and it means living together, coming together into a community. It is found in archaic communities in Greece at about this time. It is usually the result of a localized rise in population that makes villages and communities in proximity to each other but are separate from each other coalesce into a single entity.

In the 1930s, spectacular finds were made on the Palatine Hill. Excavations there revealed holes. What is spectacular about holes? They were postholes carved into the rock of one of the outcrops from the Palatine Hill. The postholes conformed to a model of an early wooden hut into which these posts would have been placed. The hut is made from the posts being placed in the ground, then the walls built around the posts and the roof put over the top of the posts. From the burials in Latium, we can tell what these huts look like. These ancient peoples of Latium liked to bury their dead (they would cremate them) in urns shaped like the houses that they lived in. They are called hut urns. What you can see if you examine a photograph of one of these hut urns, is that it has a distinctive type of roof, sort of vaguely oval-shaped. Other examples, or models, of these huts have been found that show the posts in the walls. When this is added to the postholes on the Palatine, they come together. From this, we seem to have found evidence of the first settlement in Rome. This is what the archaeologists of the 1930s felt. It is worth bearing in mind who was ruling Italy in the 1930s and why it is that they might have wanted to find evidence of the earliest settlement in Rome, but that is a different matter.

The dating of these huts on the Palatine was set at about 750 B.C. If you remember that legends say that Rome was founded by Romulus and Remus in 753 B.C., well the story of Romulus and Remus is confirmed by finding a settlement of huts on the Palatine Hill. Also, interestingly, we hear from ancient Britain sources, later sources, that the Romans themselves maintained on the Palatine, a reed and stick hut, which they called the hut of Romulus. They maintained a little shrine cared for by priests of this ancient hut that was surrounded by all kinds of magnificent buildings in later years, but the site itself was always preserved as the original house of Romulus. We are told by our ancient source, in this case a man called Dionysius of Halicarnassus, that if ever the hut collapsed or was damaged, it would always be rebuilt with the same materials that it had originally been built in. So, you put it all together, and the archaeologists of the time thought, well, here you go, we have the hut of Romulus. Do we?

The archaeological evidence then in sum gives a somewhat different picture if we look at the whole of it from the stories of the legends. What we have is a picture not of instantaneous or immediate settlement as the legends would have us believe. (Romulus decides to go out and found a town and goes out and does it on a virgin spot.) Rather, the archaeology paints a picture of gradual settlement, settlement over a total of 800 years—maybe, the place being used as a staging post for trade originally, then gradually attracting settlement, those settlements being separate villages on the hill, which eventually coalesced at some unknown period into a single community. It is a gradual evolutionary process rather than the single foundation of a town as the legend would have us believe. I think it is more important to appreciate that the problem with the archaeology vs. the legendary evidence goes deeper than that. It goes to the very soul and heart of the limits of our ancient material. We have, on the one hand, stories—wonderful and entertaining. We have on the other hand postholes, potshards, burial urns and signs of settlement. In some ways, never the twain shall meet.

Just because Aeneas had been worshipped at Lavinium in the fourth century B.C., does not confirm the Aeneas legend. All it tells us is that the people of Lavinium in the fourth century B.C. worshipped Aeneas.

It was supposed to have been around 800 years earlier. Just because we have simple looking huts on the Palatine Hill that appear to date to the eighth century B.C., does not tell us that Romulus and Remus were sent in a basket down the River Tiber, suckled by a she-wolf, found by a shepherd and rose to prominence at Alba Longa. In other words, archaeology cannot confirm legends. It cannot confirm them. In fact, more recent studies of the huts on the Palatine show that in their earliest phases they may go back to about 1000 B.C. themselves, maybe 900 B.C. So even the date of them as coinciding with the date of the stories about Romulus and Remus can now be called into question.

To a certain degree, asking archaeology to confirm this or that legend is not only unfair to archaeology, it is also unfair to the legend. After all, the function of these stories is not so much for the ancients themselves to give an accurate historical account of their past, rather to give them a shared sense of communal belonging, of origin, through which they could say, "We are all ultimately the sons of Romulus and the sons of Aeneas. We are all ultimately descendents of Troy and the Trojans." That is the most important thing about the legends, not whether or not Romulus or Remus lived, not whether the archaeology can confirm or not these ancient stories, but that they served a very important function for the ancients themselves. These stories were colorful stories of their past.

I should point out that while the archaeological evidence cannot confirm legendary evidence, it certainly has the power to disprove it. For instance, if we go back to the Aeneas, Romulus and Remus cycle, what do we have? We have Aeneas founding Lavinium. When? It would have been around 1100 B.C., some time after the Trojan War given his wanderings across the Mediterranean. Then, we have Aeneas' son Ascanius founding Alba Longa in Latium at some stage after that, perhaps 30, 40 or 50 years later. If you want to take an extreme, 50 years after Aeneas, Alba Longa is founded. Then, we have Romulus and Remus some 400 years after that founding the site of Rome. Archaeology can go to these sites and examine the archaeological record at all of these sites. It is quite clear that Lavinium and Alba Longa are not markedly older than Rome. There is no evidence that Alba Longa was around for 400 years before the site of Rome was. As a result, it seems most likely that these stories are, in their current form, cultural constructions of the later Romans to explain their origins. The historical truth was really of little interest to the Romans themselves. They simply believed them as being valuable tools to explain their ancient past, and we should approach them in the same way.

That is the story of the foundation of Rome. It is a very useful test case to examine the relative merits of archaeological evidence over written and legend, especially legendary evidence. I will not be harping on the issue of the limitation of archaeological evidence throughout the entire course. We can put that theme to bed now. It is certainly a good example and a good place to end with a theme that we brought up at the start of this course about the various limitations that are placed upon us by the ancient evidence. As a result, when we look back on those stories, we should appreciate them for what they were as far as the Romans were concerned, appreciate them as communal legends of a shared origin.

Looking ahead at the period that is known as the Regal Period, the period of the kings initiated by Romulus in legend, we can continue to say that the sources for Roman history for this very early period are very dubious indeed. The written evidence we have is from Livy. He is our main written source. The question is what sources did he have available to him? Here he is writing a history of a period as remote to him as the early Middle Ages are to us. Where is he getting his information? This raises all kinds of interesting historic-graphical questions that we can't go into in great detail, but I suppose the fairest answer to offer is that Livy was reporting legends, many of them preserved within major, noble, aristocratic houses in Rome itself, and also shared by the community. Many of the stories about the kings as we will see in more detail in the next lecture, are of this legendary character. The individual reigns of each of the seven kings of Rome (Seven is that magical number, and there are seven kings of Rome,) have a particular character to them that reflects the legendary nature of evidence. To look even further ahead I can say that the hard evidence for Roman history only starts to get really good in the period around the first Punic War in 264 B.C.

For the first 500-odd years of Roman history, our evidence is very patchy indeed. We have archaeology, but the literary material is patchy and questionable. As a result, the debates among modern scholars about many of the issues we are going to be discussing over the next few lectures are very intense. The interpretations are more divergent than they are for the later period.

Lecture Five
The Kings of Rome

Scope:

According to later tradition, Rome was initially ruled by kings. In this lecture we examine the traditions about the kings of Rome, from Romulus to Tarquinius Superbus. We see how the sources for this period are scant and difficult to use, and we note how the kings were "used" in later traditions to explain Rome's early formation in various spheres. Finally, we examine the problem of the Etruscan "domination" of Rome under the last three kings.

Outline

I. All Roman sources agree that Rome was ruled initially by kings.

    A. There were well-formed later traditions about the kings.

        1. There were seven kings in the so-called Regal Period, 753–509 B.C. They were, in order: Romulus, Numa Pompilius, Tullius Hostilius, Ancius Marcius (the Latin or Sabine Kings), Tarquinius Priscus, Servius Tullius, Tarquinius Superbus (the two Tarquins were Etruscans).

        2. Each king had a set of stories attached to him.

    B. The sources available to our main account of the early period in Livy were scant.

        1. Livy had access to now-lost written accounts by earlier writers; all, however, were far later than the Regal Period.

        2. There were received legends.

        3. Some archival and epigraphic material may have survived for Livy, but not for us.

        4. Family histories also filled out the picture.

        5. For the modern scholar, comparative material from other early monarchies is available, as well as archaeological investigation of early Rome.

    C. The operation of Roman kingship was noteworthy.

        1. The kings were not hereditary but chosen by election from among a council of nobles (the senate).

        2. Between kings, an *interrex* held office.

        3. Kings had authority over three areas of government: military affairs, administration of justice, and religion.

II. The existence of the kings themselves is not in doubt, but the historicity of the individual reigns is much more troublesome.

    A. There is little doubt about the overall veracity of the Regal Period.

        1. The ancient written sources are unanimous about the existence of the Regal Period.

        2. The earliest Latin stone inscription from the sixth century B.C., on the Black Stone in the Roman Forum, mentions a king (*rex*).

        3. Comparative analysis with other (Greek, Etruscan) polities suggests that kings regularly ruled early archaic communities.

    B. The details, however, are much more questionable.

        1. Too few kings rule over too many years (seven kings for 245 years).

        2. The stories surrounding the kings are moral dramas or etiological tales more than historical accounts.

        3. The names of some of the kings themselves raise some suspicions.

        4. Kings' "functions" are suspicious.

        5. Archaeological evidence suggests an elaboration of Rome in the period c. 625–500 B.C.; this may be the real Regal Period.

III. The last kings of Rome are traditionally seen as "Etruscan." This view has been recently challenged.

    A. The traditional view was that the Etruscans conquered Rome, hence the Etruscan kings.

    B. More recently, this view has been challenged in favor of an Etruscan influence on Rome that was not in the form of political domination. Rome remained predominantly Latin with Etruscan families gaining influence there, as they did elsewhere, but there was no "Etruscan" period as such.

Essential Reading:

Livy, *The Early History of Rome*, book 1.

T. J. Cornell, *The Beginnings of Rome*, chapters 5–6.

Supplemental Reading:

R. M. Ogilvie, *Early Rome and the Etruscans*, chapters 5–6.

Questions to Consider:

1. How reliable are the legends about the kings of Rome? What methods are available to us for checking the "facts" about early Rome?

2. How valid is the critique of the "traditional" view of Etruscan Rome? Which view—the traditional or the revisionist—do you find more compelling and why?

Lecture Five—Transcript
The Kings of Rome

Welcome back to Lecture Five of The History of Rome with The Teaching Company. Last time we reviewed stories about the foundation of Rome, the traditions the Romans told themselves about the foundation of their city, and we ended the lecture with a brief look ahead into the period that is known as the Regal Period, the period when kings ruled Rome which is traditionally said to run from 753 B.C. to 509 [B.C.]. It is on that period that I wish to focus our attention today in this lecture.

First of all, we'll review the traditions that the Romans told about the seven kings that were supposed to have ruled in this period. Then, we will recap in a little more detail an issue that we raised briefly at the end of the last lecture, which is the nature of the sources for this regal period, particularly the sources that were available to our sources, i.e. what ancient sources were available to our main author Livy who was writing about the early period. We'll then note something of the general characteristics of Roman kingship as it is handed down in these traditions. Then, we will turn our attention to the more heated question of what the historicity is of these stories. How reliable are these traditions? What do scholars say about these stories? We'll end in even more troubled waters with the issue of Etruscan Rome, raising once more the ugly question of whether the Etruscans conquered and controlled Rome.

All our sources are unanimous that Rome was initially ruled by kings. They number the kings as seven, the first one being Romulus. Romulus was we saw the founder of Rome. He also became its first king. He helped consolidate the city in various ways. He initiates wars with the immediate neighbors of the Romans, particularly the people known as the Sabines who he invites to a party in Rome and then robs all their women in an event known as the Rape of the Sabine Women, because it seemed there was a dearth of females in the fledgling state, and Romulus figured this was a good way to solve the problem. This rather impetuous act caused war with the Sabines, and then eventually peace. A peace treaty was reached between Romulus and the king of the Sabines. The Sabines were incorporated into the Roman ethnic body. There is a tradition then, at the very foundation of Rome, there is some sort of an ethnic meld between the Romans themselves who founded the town from Alba

Longa and the locals, the Sabines who were there when they showed up, which makes for an interesting situation. Romulus, upon his death becomes a god. He ascends into heaven and enters the Pantheon of Roman Gods as the founder of the Roman people.

The second king in our traditional line of kings is a man called Numa Pompilius. There is a name for your first born. Numa Pompilius is presented to us as having essentially created all of Rome's religious institutions. He founds a whole variety of major cults and colleges of priests who are very powerful and prominent in later Roman society. Chief among these priests, and we will be hearing a lot about these particular men, are the pontificates, the pontiffs, who are the chief college of pagan priests in ancient Rome. There are others. I won't bore you with the details, but there are others all of whom Numa Pompilius is supposed to have established during his reign.

Following the religious zeal of Numa Pompilius comes Tullius Hostilius, the aggressive Tullius. He lives up to his name because he goes around bashing up on Rome's neighbors in no short order. He destroys Alba Longa, which is the mother city of the Romans, if you want to think of it that way. After all, the line of Romulus had come from Alba Longa, now, the new state of Rome goes out and destroys the mother city in its expansion into Latium. Lots of other Latin neighbors of the Romans suffer under the aggressive policies of Tullius Hostilius in the tradition, and he helps expand Rome's borders, beginning the long process of conquest of the Latins.

The fourth king is known as Ancius [variant spelling Ancus] Marcius. He is presented in the wake of the actions of Tullius Hostilius as more of a consolidator. He founds colonies, specifically and most importantly, the colony at Ostia at the mouth of the Tiber on the sea, which was to become Rome's chief port. Rome is not on the sea. It is on the Tiber, inland, and Ostia is down at the estuary of the Tiber River. Ancius Marcius is supposed to have founded that colony which is to become a very important place in later Roman history. There are other places that he founds as well. He basically goes around building on the achievements of Tullius Hostilius. For instance, he bridges the Tiber. He is the first one to put a bridge across the Tiber. That is the sort of thing that Ancius Marcius does.

These first four kings are often called the Latin or Sabine kings. They all seem to have derived from the native community of now the Romans and their Sabine partners. The last three kings of Rome (or at least two of the last three kings of Rome) are of a different origin. Two of them are called Tarquinius. Tarquinius Priscus is the fifth king, and Tarquinius Superbus is the seventh and final king. Between them is a man called Servius Tullius who is not of the same ethnic origin as Tarquinius Priscus and Superbus. Why do I talk about Tarquinius? I do so because Tarquinius means "the man from Tarquinii, which is an Etruscan town. The tradition about Tarquinius Priscus is that he was originally called Lucomo, a man from Tarquinii who moved to Rome and established himself and his family as a prominent force in Rome and eventually become king there. In other words Tarquinius Priscus is an Etruscan. These three kings are often called the Etruscan kings, or at least the period of Etruscan control in Rome. This is some of the chief evidence for those who believe in the Etruscan period of Roman history.

It must be said that the ancients themselves show considerable confusion over the traditions of Tarquinius Priscus and Tarquinius Superbus. Tarquinius Priscus just means the first Tarquin, the prior Tarquin. Tarquinius Superbus means the arrogant Tarquin, more about him in a second. They show quite a bit of confusion between the two. In some cases, they seem to do much of the same sort of thing. Basically, what they seem to do is a lot of building. They construct things. Tarquinius Priscus starts building a massive temple to Jupiter on the Capitoline Hill, which will become the national temple of the national guard of the Romans. He is the one who started this project of a big temple to the national guard of the Romans. He also initiated a variety of other building programs. We hear from Livy that the people grumbled at this because they were forced to labor in peace time as hard as they labored in war time. Tarquinius Priscus, whatever the shady details of his reign, basically is presented as a more sophisticated sort of king, a king involved more in the construction and consolidation of the city of Rome. He is followed by Servius Tullius, a man of obscure origin. His name would suggest that he had some slave background (the Latin word for slave is *servus*) and there is a tradition that he was the son of a slave woman. He became king following Tarquinius Priscus, and he is presented to us as a social and military reformer, basically out of the reign of Servius Tullius, in the Roman tradition, came all Rome's social and military institutions. Like that, they were all invented in the space of about 40 years by one guy. Maybe we are beginning to get a sense of how the kings operated in Roman tradition.

Servius Tullius dies a bad death in a *coup d'etat* and is replaced by Tarquinius Superbus, who is the son of Tarquinius Priscus and has been waiting in the wings for many years. He takes over the throne. As his name supplies, Tarquinius—Tarquin the Arrogant—he behaves as a tyrant. He increases the toil placed upon the Romans by building bigger and more grandiose projects. He behaves in an arrogant fashion. He arbitrarily issues judgments against people. He executes senators who are in disagreement. Basically, he behaves as any tyrant in the classical tradition behaves. He is a typical tyrant. As a result of his behavior and the behavior of his son in the lecture after next, he is ousted and thrown out of Rome. As a result, the Regal Period comes to an end and is replaced with the Republic, but more on that later.

There are your seven kings, then, and it is worth asking, how do we know any of this and how did the Romans know it? As I say, our chief source is Livy. He had available to him earlier writers who are not available to us. I must stress all of the earlier writers that he had available to him were far later than the Regal Period. There were no extant literary sources available to Livy that were contemporary with the Regal Period. What else did he use? He would have used the established legends, the communal legends and stories of the Romans, what the Romans told about their regal and monarchic past—general communal legends. There would have been some archiving and epigraphic material as well. We know that the pontificates—the pontiffs—of Rome kept records of signs, omens and prodigies from the gods. These were kept in the pontifical archive, and appear to have attached to them notices of major historical events year by year. "In the year that these signs were seen, when this, this and this happened," and so forth. So, as a result, it is possible that Livy would have had access to those pontifical archives. How far they went, what they were like, we have none of that. How far they went, what they were like, and how reliable they are is a different issue. There may also have been some epigraphic materials, inscriptions that Livy may have looked at. Again, its quantity and value are very hard to assess because we don't have much of it. We have a little stone, a scrap of pottery as well, with some inscription on it, but how extensive, detailed and informative this was we can't say. The final form of a source that Livy would have had available to him would have been family histories, the histories of individuals in aristocratic houses of Rome, who, as you will see, revered their ancestors. Livy could have discussed the family histories with the individuals of his day and perhaps get information about the distant past. Again, the quality of that information we cannot check.

We have available to us, unlike Livy, the material of archaeology as well as comparative data from other early so-called archaic societies that allow us to at least see how typical or atypical the Roman kings were in relation to how we know other early societies and their kingships. So, you put it all together, and we can at least check out these stories. That is what we are going to do. We are going to see how scholars assess the historicity, the truth or lack of truth in some of these tales. Before I do that, however, there are some general characteristics of Roman kingship that are clear from these traditions that we should note. They are interesting and we will see them again in the future. They will rear themselves in various shapes in the future of this course.

First of all, the kings of Rome are not a family tree. It is not a dynasty that passed on from father to son. Kingship is not a hereditary quality in Rome. What happens is that at the end of a king's reign, a council of noblemen, whom the Romans call senators, came together and chose one from among their number. Then an election took place, and the new king was ratified by a vote of the people. If this process went on for a long period, a man called an *interrex*—*Rex* means king in Latin, so an *interrex* means a man between the king (just an example of how logical and structured the Latin language is)—came forward and helped organize the elections and took the nominations to choose the next king. That is an important point. The kingship of ancient Rome was not a hereditary institution. It was one that was rather passed around among the landowning aristocracy.

Finally, the kings themselves, like most ancient kings, seem to have held authority over three areas. They were the chief military leaders of the State. In times of war, they were the ones who led the military, made treaties and decided on tactics and strategies. They were also the chief judicial bodies of the state. They were the ones who issued judgments. In the case of the likes of Tarquinius, they were arbitrary and tyrannical judgments. They are basically the font of law at this stage, and finally, they are the chief bridge between humans and gods. They are the chief religious authorities of the state. The military, judicial, and religious branches of society are all controlled by kings. This is something that has parallels in other cultures.

How true are these tales? How reliable are any of these stories? Save for the most extreme skeptic, there are no mainstream scholars who doubt the overall veracity of the Regal Period. There are no scholars who doubt that the period of the kings actually took place. In the first place, the Roman authors are absolutely unanimous that they were ruled by kings. There is not a single dissenting voice that says, "We were never ruled by kings, we started off as a republic." Everyone agreed that there was a period when Rome was ruled by kings. Secondly, our earliest Latin stone inscription which is to be found in the Roman forum (it can be seen today) our earliest extant stone inscription in Latin (written in quasi-Greek letters but in the Latin language) called "the black stone" dates to about the sixth century B.C. It is fragmentary. We can't read it. It might as well be a recipe for scrambled eggs for all we know. If it is a recipe for scrambled eggs, it is the recipe for a king's scrambled eggs, because the word king, "rex," appears in the inscription. That is very interesting. Secondly, an even more dramatic epigraphic evidence became unearthed when excavations took place in the area known as the *reggia* in the Roman Forum. (The *reggia* means the king's house. This was traditionally the place where the king lived.) Excavations took place there, and they dug down and found very early buildings, going back as early as the sixth century B.C. In amongst the finds was a scrap of pottery. The pottery is called *bucchero*, a type of Etruscan pottery. Written on that pottery is one word, *rex*, king. This is extremely dramatic evidence found inside the king's house, written on an Etruscan piece of pottery in the sixth century B.C. is the word king.

As I say comparative data with other sources would seem to suggest that this model of kingship, as it has come down to us in the traditions from ancient Rome, is not something that, in itself, we would question. From the Greeks and the Etruscans, we do see early contemporary societies at this time ruled by kings, which then move away from kingship into a form of oligarchy just as the Roman state was to do at the end of the Regal Period.

Broadly speaking, most scholars would be agreed that when you put all this evidence together—it is not unproblematic evidence; a lot of it can be questioned. Some people argue that the *rex* of the inscriptions that I have just mentioned is not the king but a man called a *rex sacrorum*, king of sacred rights whom we know existed in the Post-Regal Period in the Republic—that there was a monarchic regal period of Roman history. It is the details that are problematic. Were there seven kings? The fact that the number of kings of Rome is seven is itself worrisome. Seven is one of those magical, special numbers in the Mediterranean culture. Seven and three have special significance. Seven kings? It seems too neat. The Regal Period stretches by tradition from 753 B.C. to 509 B.C. if we count inclusively, that is 245 years. Seven kings ruling over 245 years gives an average of 35 years per king. That is a longer average per reign than any historically documented dynasty anywhere. Even for some of the most stable, such as the dynasty that is still in control in England, 35 years is exceptionally long. That is cause for concern, and scholars looking at that fact come to one of two logical conclusions. Either there were more kings who have dropped out of the picture to reach the number seven, that special number, or there were seven kings, but the Regal Period is shorter. It was not 245 years. Both sides have been argued and can be argued cogently.

Second, looking at the kings themselves, the stories surrounding the kings read more like moral tales and etiological tales (tales that describe the origins of things) than they do like actual historical events. For example, the story of Servius Tullius' removal from power goes something like this. Servius had a rather evil daughter, Tullia by name, who began an adulterous affair with the son of Tarquinius Priscus (i.e. Tarquin the younger, who was later to become Tarquin the Arrogant.) This villainous couple then murdered Servius and seized power for themselves. The purpose of the story is as much didactic as anything else. It is a model of bad behavior for the Romans. Tullia is a person who is thoroughly evil. She carries out appalling and atrocious acts in Roman eyes. She cheats on her husband, disrespecting the family institution. She murders people, and she disrespects her father which is by Roman standards one of the worst things that you can do. She so disrespects him, says Livy, that she runs over his body in a chariot as it is lying on the street. And, says Livy, this happens to be the same street that today is called Criminal Street as a result of that act.

So, what we seem to have then in the stories about the kings are really moral tales, nice stories that offer up examples of honorable and dishonorable behavior and as well help explain the origin of things. I have mentioned the issue of the street, but if we look at the broader functions of the kings themselves, there is cause for concern there. All the kings have specific agendas. Tullius Hostilius is the aggressive Tullius who goes out and beats up on Rome's Latin neighbors. Numa Pompilius is the guy who invents all of Rome's religious institutions, establishing all of the colleges of priests and most of the main cults of ancient Rome. Servius Tullius constructs Rome's social and military institutions. So, in some ways, the kings appear to be like pegs. They appear to be pegs upon which later Romans would hang the origins of things. "Where did the priesthood called Salius come from?" "Oh, Numa Pompilius was the religious king. He must have invented it." "How is it that we have a system of centuries that our army is organized into?" "Servius Tullius was the social and military reformer. That must be where that came from."

The kings are sort of like pigeon holes into which the later Romans could put the origins and aspects of later Roman history and society. The names of the kings themselves are suspicious. Numa Pompilius: Pompilius seems to be related to the Latin word *pompa* which means a religious procession. Here he is, Numa, the religious procession guy, and he is involved in establishing Rome's religious institutions. We have Tullius Hostilius, hostile Tullius, Tullius the aggressive, and he is a warmonger. We have Tarquinius Priscus, the first Tarquin, which seems to assume that there will be a second Tarquin. As far as archaeological evidence goes, we have bits and pieces of early Rome. The situation with regard to the archaeology of early Rome is very difficult of course. Rome has always been occupied. You can't just go and plow up all the later imperial and republican city and try to get back to the earliest levels of the city. Bits and pieces of it have been found and we do have some monuments from the very earliest period including a sewer, the *cloaca maxima*, the great sewer of Rome, which can still be seen today. I am showing you a photograph of it I took recently on the River Tiber. You can actually go down and take an even closer photograph of it. Much of what you see if you go there today is a fourth century reconstruction of the *cloaca*. If you go inside, which I did not do, but people have ventured inside, then you can see the original sixth century masonry inside that is still in use.

There are signs that Rome in this early period around 600 B.C. or thereabouts is undergoing quite a lot of urban development. This would be consistent with a monarchic type rule, especially an

Etruscan monarchic rule, which raises the question about the Etruscans. Naturally, those people who see an Etruscan period of Roman history are those who see a wider Etruscan dominance in central Italy at this time. According to this view, the Tarquinian dynasty, the two Tarquins represent the takeover of Rome by the Etruscans, in other words, the foreign occupation of this city by the Etruscans. We do find Etruscan pottery in Rome. We also find Etruscan style statuary in some of the earliest levels of Rome made of clay in the Etruscan style. The Romans had a tradition themselves that the Etruscans came from Etruria. According to this model, then it is clear evidence of the Etruscan period of Roman history.

Whereas I mentioned the wider Etruscan control of central Italy has been called into question, and if that is called into question, then the Etruscan period of Rome must be called into question. What is the nature of the control of the Tarquins over Rome? The tradition is clear that Tarquinius Priscus formerly called Lucomo, came from the town of Tarquinii but came with his wife. He did not come with an army. He came with his wife, moved into the community of Rome and made himself a man of importance to his wealth, charm and aggressive canvassing for his own position and eventually became king through the process of his own election. This used to be more in line with what we know generally about archaic societies in which aristocratic people can move between communities with relative degrees of freedom.

The connections between aristocrats in these early societies, the personal connection between them, seems to have been more important than their individual citizenship. On the model of the looser Etruscan control of Rome, what we have is evidence in the archaeology for Etruscan cultural influence in the city, absolutely, and evidence that an Etruscan family became dominant at some stage and was remembered as having become dominant, but that we are not talking about the occupation of Rome by a foreign power. We are not talking about the Etruscans conquering the city of Rome, rather an Etruscan family rising to prominence from the community of Rome having come in from outside. Again, whether that view is going to be widely accepted is still to be seen.

So much for the Regal Period and the stories of the kings. Much of what I have told you is hotly debated. I have tried to outline at least the main thrusts of the scholarly debates that are ongoing about this subject. Fundamentally, the issue of what you believe or don't believe about this period boils down to a simple question. How much do you believe the written sources? Some scholars like to believe that the written sources are certainly legendary and do not tell a straightforward historical fact. But, I would like to say they must reflect something of an historical past. They must reflect some communal memory of these kings and their reigns. It is a matter of degree how much you are going to accept. Some scholars say all the legends are complete nonsense and have nothing to do with history. We should only look at the archaeology. Forget the written legends and stories. Nice though they might be, they are not historical. It is really a matter of degree, and one has to orient oneself on a spectrum of opinion. You have to do that by reading lots of Livy and lots of modern scholarship on the subject.

Next time, we will look at the society, as far as we can reconstruct it, of this earliest period of Roman history.

Lecture Six
Regal Society

Scope:

In this lecture we examine the shape of early Roman society as reconstructed from available evidence. Several features of late Roman society, it seems, were already in evidence in the very earliest period of Roman history. We also examine the shape of government and politics on the eve of the Republic's foundation.

Outline

I. Regal society at Rome was dominated by aristocratic landowners, with those below them tied by bonds of favor and obligation.

    A. Early Roman society was typically archaic, which includes the existence of slavery.

        1. Among the freeborn population, the broadest distinction was that between citizen and non-citizen.

        2. All citizens were grouped into units called "tribes." Initially there were three tribes, but in later centuries they reached a total of thirty-five.

        3. One of the chief duties of citizenship was military service in the Roman army, which fought in the phalanx formation at this early date.

        4. As with contemporary societies in Greece, the citizenry was led primarily by aristocratic landowning families.

        5. All families, it seems, were grouped into clans (*gens, gentes*).

        6. The so-called "three names" of Roman citizens reflects the primacy of the *gens* in the familial and social order.

    B. Prominent families and common families were tied by a system called *clientela*.

        1. The social system of clientship *(clientela)* was in operation.

        2. A patron granted favors and generally helped a client, and in return he received support, loyalty, and due deference and respect.

        3. *Clientela* helped offset the horizontal stratification of Roman society. However, not all classes or persons were involved in the *clientela* system.

II. At this early date it is possible that the first social "Orders" appeared.

    A. In Roman society an "Order" was a social rank, a statement of status.

        1. The first Order to appear seems to have been the Patriciate.

        2. Patricians were defined by birth, and thus by their names; they were the most privileged group within the aristocracy.

        3. The circumstances surrounding the emergence of the patricians are obscure; various reconstructions have been offered by modern scholars.

        4. Whether or not the other social Order, the Plebs, was in existence in this early period is not clear.

III. Politics under the Regal system of government was controlled by the aristocrats more by than the kings.

    A. Kings were chosen from among the members of the senate and ratified by the people, i.e., the adult male citizens meeting in assembly.

        1. The status of the senate in this very early period is unclear; it may have been an *ad hoc* council of advisors to the king.

        2. The people were grouped into voting units called *curiae* and met in an assembly called the Curiate Assembly *(comitia curiata)*. There are parallels to this in Greek and other archaic cultures.

        3. The main function of the Curiate Assembly was to ratify the senate's choice of a new king and officially to confer the power of command *(imperium)* upon him.

    B. Brief consideration of the so-called "Servian Constitution" (after Servius Tullius) illustrates many of the problems in dealing with the Regal Period.

        1. Many of the features of the system are clearly anachronistic, but some may date to the Regal Period.

        2. The difficulty lies in determining which ones do.

Essential Reading:

T. J. Cornell, *The Beginnings of Rome*, chapters 4, 7, 10.

Supplemental Reading:

G. Alföldi, *The Social History of Rome*, esp. chapter 1.

Questions to Consider:

1. Is it valid to infer the existence and operation of certain social and political institutions at an early date, for which we have no contemporary ancient evidence, from an examination of their form at a later date, for which we do? If not, what alternatives are open to us?

2. On what criteria was Roman society stratified into social classes? What was the function of *clientela*?

Lecture Six—Transcript
Regal Society

Hello again and welcome to the sixth lecture in The History of Ancient Rome. Last time we looked at the traditions concerning the kings of Rome (seven in number according to the stories) and we also examined the hotly debated question, of how believable and historical those traditional stories about the kings are. I leave the final decision on that difficult issue to you all individually. I want to move on today to examine the shape of this early Roman society. There are many features of later Roman society that the Romans themselves considered to be very old, very ancient, and which most scholars would accept were very old and may go back to this very early phase of Roman history, may go back to the Regal Period. That is what I want to focus on today. I want to look first of all at the general shape of Roman society, which we will see was typically archaic, that is to say, typical for a period of around 600 B.C. to 500 B.C. Then, we will look at some of the peculiar aspects of Roman society that were really unique in many ways to the Romans themselves. Then, we will look at the broad shape of politics, as it seems to have been played out at this early period. We will end by taking an example, the so-called Servian constitution or Servian Reforms, which we will use to show the kinds of difficulties we have interpreting the data as we have it for this early period of Roman society.

The Regal Society of Rome was typically archaic. It was dominated by aristocratic landowners. There seems to have been from the start a division between free and slave. It seems that the Romans were a slaving society from very early on as were most societies as we will see when we come to look at the depressing question of slavery in ancient Rome. It is unfortunately the case that most societies in human history have been slaving societies. They don't seem to have been particularly numerous, the slaves in this period of early Rome, but there was a division between freeborn and slave. That is the most basic division that seems to have existed in this early society. Within the freeborn population, there was a distinction between the citizen and the non-citizen. Throughout this entire course, when I say citizen, I will be referring to the adult male population of Rome who are enfranchised, allowed to vote and take part in the political process, and various judicial and legal rights that non-citizens did not possess. The citizen body of ancient Rome was always a restricted body of all male citizens. Excluded were all women, slaves, and any foreigners who had come to Rome and were not members of the citizen body—i.e. alien residents.

This citizen body appears from earliest time to have been divided into units called tribes. Again, this terminology is quite difficult. I am not referring to the tribal societies we talked about when we looked at pre-Roman Italy, the non-urbanized tribal societies like the Samnites in central Italy. These units are called tribes because the Latin word is *tribus*. It appears to be derived from the word "three." It appears to mean "by threes." This would make sense since we hear that the Roman citizen body was initially divided into three units called tribes. These seem to have been voting units used for the constitution of a popular assembly for the purposes of voting. They are called tribes, although the terminology is a wee bit confusing since we have looked at tribal societies, but that is not what I am talking about here. When I talk about the citizen tribes or the voting tribes, I am talking about these divisions of citizens into voting units.

There were three of these tribes from the earliest times. One of the chief duties of citizenship that fell upon all citizens was military service. If you had privileges as a citizen, you had obligations. Among those obligations in all archaic societies high up on the list is military service. If the call to arms comes, you collect your equipment, because you are not supplied by the state, and you show up on the appointed day, enroll in the army and go off and fight whoever it is. If you happen to be a citizen under Tullius Hostilius, then it seems you spent quite a lot of your summer time in the fields beating up on your neighbors.

It seems that the Romans at this very early stage fought in the formation called the phalanx, which is a Greek style, tightly packed body of heavily armored soldiers with large round shields, using spears predominantly as an offensive weapon. The idea of a phalanx is to advance on your enemy in a single mass and quite literally shove them off the field. It is when the opposing army breaks that most of the killing is done. There is a period of shoving, then when the other line breaks you do a lot of the killing. More of that when we come to look at Roman warfare and the Roman army. In other archaic societies, particularly those that are better documented like in Greece, it seems that the land owning, wealthy families dominated this early society. These families and all the common families as well were grouped into units we call clans. The Latin word is *gens* or *gentes*, and they have been translated into English as clans. These are very unclear units for us today. It is very hard to appreciate where this idea came from. We know that the clans were often organized around a particular religious tribe. It may have been a religious grouping at its soul, but it is really hard to make out where this organization came from. When we are talking about a clan, we are talking about a group of families who share a name and are identified as members of X or Y clan. The origins of this clan system are obscure, and its functions are obscure, but it seems that all Roman citizen body members were members of clans, some of them prominent, some less prominent.

I mentioned this issue of the Roman name, it is worth bringing that into play now, because the Roman name reflects the dominance of the clan system. Traditionally, your typical Roman citizen would have three names. To take an example Lucius Cornelius Sulla, would be a typical Roman name. The name actually is more than just an identification like Joe Smith. The name identifies you in the social cosmos, it locates you in the Roman hierarchical social order. The most important name of the three names of the Roman is the middle one. It is called the Name. It is sometimes called the Clan Name. This, in the case of Lucius Cornelius Sulla, tells us that that person is a member of the Cornelian clan. That is a prominent, important clan. You know immediately in hearing that name this is a person of importance. The name in front of the Clan Name is called the *pre-nomen*, which means "in front." That is the name that identifies you as an individual—Lucius. So, with Lucius Cornelius, we get the information that you are the individual Lucius of the clan Cornelius. The Romans had very few of these forenames, so few that they are often abbreviated by single letters. Lucius, for instance, is L., Titus is T., Marcus is M., Quintus is Q, and so forth. There were actually very few of those names. They weren't particularly imaginative when it came to naming people, at least not individuals. The *pre-nomen* is the name that indicates your individual identity within the clan. The third name seems originally to have been a nickname that was added on to certain branches of a clan and so was identified as a family name. So, you have Lucius Cornelius Sulla is Lucius, from the clan Cornelius of the family Sulla that is in the clan Cornelius. You could also have another guy called Publius Cornelius Scipio. He is the individual Publius, in the same clan Cornelius, but of the family Scipio. Different family, same clan. The point that I am driving home here is that it is the clan name that is the key. That is the one that is called The Name. The other two names are in reference to it.

One of the features of Roman society from this early period that was to live on throughout Roman history is a rather odd feature of Roman society. It is the system called "clientship," *clientela* in the Latin. When I explain this to my students, I like to draw on an image from modern movies to explain how clientship works. Basically, clientship is a system of favor granting which is based on an obligation placed on the person to whom the favor has been granted. I'll scratch your back if you scratch mine. That is the fundamental nature of it. It is a system of reciprocal arrangements between people. The image I like to give my students is the opening scene of *The Godfather*. We have Don Corleone sitting passively in his study with various catering lowlies brought before him to ask favors, and he either imperiously grants or denies their requests. If he grants the request, they are then under an obligation to him. It is a criminal obligation, and I am not saying that ancient clientship was one big mafia organization, but the essence of that relationship that is being expressed in *The Godfather*, is really what clientship is about.

You go to someone who has influence or power to help you, you ask them for a favor (that is the literal Latin word *beneficium,* a benefit, a favor) and once that is done, you are under an *obligatio,* or obligation, to support them or do whatever it is that they want you to do. It might be political support, build a barn on the farm, whatever. When the time comes for you to pay back the favor, you do it. You become the client of a patron. The person granting the favor is a patron. The person accepting the favor or obligation is the client. *Clientela*, clientship, helped offset the horizontal stratification in Roman society. It created vertical connections between prominent and lowly families. So, the centrifugal forces that might threaten to tear a really hierarchical society apart were somewhat offset by this system of favor granting. I should point out that inherent in the system is the expectation that the client has something to offer. You don't grant a favor to someone who can do nothing for you in return. As a result, the poorest and most destitute members of society will tend to be left out of this system. Not everyone was involved in a patron/client relationship. In many ways, it is a relationship between parties of relative degrees of influence. More influence granting helped people of lesser influence that can then be utilized when the people with more influence need it in the future.

Another feature of Roman society that appears to have gone back to the very earliest periods is the organization of people into groups called "Orders." By Orders, I am using the phrase in the Latin term *ordo,* plural *ordinaes,* which means a rank, a status, a rank within a society. By tradition, there were two orders in the very earliest periods of Roman history, the patricians and the plebeians. Most scholars are of the opinion that the plebeians didn't actually come into existence as an order until later. We look at the possible emergence of the plebeians in a later lecture. It does seem that the patricians are very old indeed and may go back to the very earliest, the Regal Period, of Roman history. The patricians were a group of clans defined by birth. In other words, your patrician status came with you with your name. It was identifiable with your name immediately. For instance, the Cornelii were all patricians. Any member of the clan Cornelius was automatically a patrician. So was the clan Julius, for instance, or the clan Claudius. Claudius was also a patrician name. Other names would automatically be recognized as non-patrician, later recognized as plebeian.

The question of where the system of patricians came from is, you won't be surprised to hear, hotly debated. Various theories have been advanced over the years, sometimes theories that reflect more the interest or inclinations of those advancing them than they do anything about the past. For instance, when racial theories of superiority were popular, what did we have? The patricians are obviously of decent Aryan hard-working stock, and the slovenly plebeians are typical Mediterranean shiftless types. Absolute nonsense. Not a shred of evidence to support any racial distinction between the patricians and the plebeians. Other views have been that the patricians were all the wealthy clans and the plebeians were the poor, in other words, that there is an economic division. That seems overly simplistic and the evidence for wealthy plebeian clans from early on in the history of the republic. So, if the plebeians were around before that, the argument goes "It is a leap that they just suddenly became wealthy out of nowhere." The economic division between plebeians and patricians seems to be a bit simplistic and naïve.

Whatever the case of the origin of these orders, it does seem that the patricians were around from the very earliest period. I reiterate the plebeians, who later are designated as every one who is not a patrician, that is a later designation, their origins, whether or not they were around as early as the patricians is a matter of considerable debate. That is unclear to us. Personally, I favor the view that the plebeians emerged slightly later after the early republic. This we will look at when we examine the so-called Struggle of the Orders of the Plebeians and Patricians in early and middle republic.

What we have then if we just pause to look at the shape of Roman society before we examine the system of politics, is already a fairly hierarchical system of social order. This will be a mark of Roman society throughout its entire history. It was originally a hierarchical social order where status determined everything. If you were a patrician, you had advantages over non-patricians. If you were a citizen, you had advantages over non-citizens. If you were freeborn, you had advantages over slaves. We are dealing with a social order that is rigidly hierarchic and was to become even more so, but which is somewhat offset by the system of clientship between people of influence.

Looking at the politics of the Regal Period, what we see is that the kings were chosen from among the Senate body and were granted their powers by ratification by popular vote. The Senate at this early stage is also much disputed. Was a standing body in the state, an ad hoc advisory council to the king, convened as needed? Or did it meet regularly? It is most unclear as to whether the Senate was a regular standing body of the state. From its ranks were chosen the next candidates for the kingship, and the vote was taken by the people who were in a popular assembly known as the *comitia curiata*, which means the curiate assembly. This is because they were organized into thirty units called *curiae* meaning a grouping so far as we can tell. *Curiae* is curious. There is no pun intended.

The *comitia curiata* is literally the meeting of the people in their *curiae*, and there were thirty of them as seems to have been the case, ten *curiae* per tribe. There were three tribes originally. The tribes were subdivided into ten units each called *curiae*, and when the vote came it was taken by blocks. Block voting. It was the *curiae* that voted, not the individuals. The individuals voted within their particular *curiae*. Then it was the curial vote that was put forward.

That is why it is called the *curiate* assembly, the assembly organized of people assembled into voting units called *curiae*. The origins of this are unclear, but we have parallels for this in Greece and other archaic societies, even in some fairly rigid and monarchic societies, popular assemblies seem to have been a feature of these early archaic societies. So, it is not surprising to find one in Rome. The *comitia curiata*, is the earliest of the popular assemblies.

When we look at the Republic, we will see that three more came to be added to that list. That is three more popular assemblies. But more of that anon. It is important to know that the main function of the *curiate* assembly is to ratify the choice of king and then to confer upon that king the power of command. This power is called *imperium* in Latin. We will be seeing a lot more of this. Pay careful attention to this concept. *Imperium* is the quality of command. It allows you to order people around. It has a very military feel to it. A general in Latin is called an *imperator*, a man who wields *imperium*, the power of command. Note that in the Roman tradition, it is the people who confer *imperium*. The people, the *populus Romanus* convened into an official assembly are the only ones who can confer the power of command on someone. That is the main function of the curiate assembly—to ratify the choice of king and confer the power of command on that king. As an aside, the word *imperium* may look vaguely familiar. It means the power of command, then it came to mean the area over which the Romans had the power to command people. So, it has come into the English language as empire. That is why we have empire and imperial (as opposed to empirial).

Some of the difficulties of trying to sort out the social and political military details of this period are nicely illustrated by consideration of the Constitution of the Servian Reforms. We saw in the last lecture how the king Servius Tullius was credited in the tradition with inventing Rome's social and military system. Livy and a contemporary source, a man called Dionysius of Halicarnassus—he wrote in Greek but about Roman antiquities—describe the Servian Constitution. In other words they ascribe this to Servius Tullius, the king who came between the two Tarquins.

What they say is as follows. They say that Servius Tullius came around and instituted a wide-ranging series of reforms. He disposed of the three original tribes of Roman people, which seem to be or may have been organized along ethnic lines. We saw that the very earliest fledgling state of Rome had adopted many Sabines into its midst. Many scholars believe this is the origin of tribes, to divide the original units of Roman society from each other ethnically. Whatever the case about that, the three original tribes are often called the Romulean tribes, the tribes established by Romulus, and were replaced by Servius Tullius, we are told, by 20 tribes now determined by location. The tribes are like parishes or boroughs. One enters a tribe by being born in or living in a certain location. These are essentially local units, and we are told he had four urban tribes and sixteen that were based in the countryside.

We are also told by Livy and Dionysius that Servius then instituted a system of classes based upon wealth. He divided the Roman citizen body (this applies to adult males only) into five classes based upon wealth. These classes organized into units called centuries which were a military organization according to our sources. They were units in the army. You would have had soldiers divided up by wealth equipped differently dependent on how they could afford to equip themselves. Finally, he used this military organization as a basis to create a new popular assembly, which was called the *comitia centuriata*, the *centuriate* assembly. The people assembled into centuries. We have the *curiate* assembly on one hand, the people assembled in their *curiae*, and now we have a new series of voting blocks, the people assembled in centuries. According to our traditions, these centuries were assigned to classes in such a way that the richer classes had an advantage. The voting is done in the voting blocks of centuries, not by individuals. If you have more centuries assigned to the numerically fewer richer people, they will have a greater advantage in the voting in that assembly. This is a complex situation. We have Servius Tullius instituting new tribes, a new military order, and then using that military order as a basis for a new political order. All of this is supposed to have come out of the head of Servius Tullius in the mid-sixth century B.C. It can be shown that this is impossible.

From the evidence of Dionysius and Livy themselves. In the year 495 B.C., these same authors who have reported the Servian Constitution tell us that in 495 B.C. two new tribes were added because of the expansion of Roman territory bringing the total to 21. I thought Servius Tullius had introduced 20 tribes. If the total went to 21 in 495 B.C., where is the missing tribe? The answer is obviously that the latter picture is the more correct one. The number of local tribes grew piecemeal incrementally in pace with the expansion of Roman territory. The idea that they just came out of Servius' head is much more unlikely. We can say that some of the names of the tribes, even the ones that were supposed to have been created by Servius Tullius, are anachronistic. One tribe is called *Tribe Claudia*, clearly named after the influential Patrician clan the Claudii, but they did not come to Rome until 504 B.C., 50 years or more after Servius Tullius. It can be shown that these details are questionable. The ancient sources have simplified a more complex evolutionary process and ascribed it all under Servius Tullius.

The division of the people into five classes is difficult because essentially five classes of centuries fight in the army. The Romans at this stage fought in the phalanx formation. What you need is a large round shield, a spear, breastplate, helmet and sword. If you can afford it, a piece of armor for your lower leg called a *greave*, the shield covering your lower thigh. You can't go into a phalanx missing a shield. You can't say, "I can afford most of the equipment, but I can't afford the spear." The division of people into five classes assumes a more complex military situation than the phalanx would seem to allow, especially since this division is accredited in our sources as being instituted for military purposes originally. Surely the only division is between those who can afford the equipment and those who can't. That is only two classes. Maybe that is what Servius Tullius did originally. He made a classification of those who could afford the equipment and those who can't. This later division into five classes reflects a more complex military order, which we know the Romans instituted toward the end of fifth century. At this point, they divided their troops into units called *maniples*, and they began to operate in a more complex fashion on the battlefield with a grade of equipment involved. The five classes of soldier much better fit that picture (i.e. a late fifth century development) than they do a mid-sixth century development. What we seem to have in our sources is a conflation of a more complex evolutionary process packed together into one single unit and presented to us as the product of a single man operating in a single brief period.

This is the broad shape of Roman society. We will see again the *comitia centuriata* when we look at the republic. It is the establishment of the republic that I will turn our attention to the next time around. I hope that some of the difficulties of trying to interpret the data for the Regal Period have been made clear to you. You can see how it is that our sources are often contradictory and once more at the heart of everything in trying to analyze this data is the issue of interpretation, argument and the presentation of contrary and competing reconstructions of events. That is the heart of ancient history as I said in lecture one, and I hope by now, everyone has that message loud and clear.

Lecture Seven
The Beginnings of the Republic

Scope:

With the expulsion of the kings in 509 B.C., Rome became a Republic governed by annually elected magistrates. In this lecture, we discuss the traditional tale of the foundation of the Republic and the criticisms leveled against it by some modern scholars. We also review how the constitution of the fledgling Republic developed, and we consider social developments that were to lead to the Struggle of the Orders.

Outline

I. In Roman tradition, the Republic was founded following an atrocious act that spurred a *coup d'état.*

  A. Tarquinius Superbus, the last king of Rome, was a poor ruler who enacted various policies that were unpopular.

  B. His son, Sextus Tarquinius, raped Lucretia, a nobleman's wife, who subsequently committed suicide. This assault sparked a coup.

   1. A family friend of Lucretia's husband, L. Junius Brutus, helped the dead woman's incensed family to organize resistance against Superbus; many members of the Tarquin clan were also part of the plot.

   2. Tarquinius was forced to abandon Rome.

   3. A plot to restore the monarchy led to Brutus having to execute his own two sons.

   4. Assisted by Lars Porsenna, king of nearby Clusium, Tarquinius attempted to regain Rome by force of arms but failed.

   5. A subsequent attack by Porsenna on the Latins failed at the Battle of Aricia (506 B.C.), and he withdrew back to Clusium.

  C. Modern scholars have treated this cycle of stories in different ways; none accept them as they are.

   1. The stories are, on the face of it, typical of the early history of Rome: romantic, heroic, and didactic.

2. Another ancient tradition records that the Romans surrendered to Porsenna and that he imposed a humiliating treaty on Rome.

D. Modern scholars, faced with these difficulties, have come up with a variety of alternative reconstructions of events, such as:

1. The expulsion of the Tarquins is to be read against the background of waning Etruscan power in Italy in the fifth century B.C.

2. The transition from monarchy to Republic was not a single, dramatic event but a slow process stretching into the mid-fifth century B.C.

3. The story of Lucretia is, in fact, not improbable, given comparable "personal" events in other royal dynasties that had broad political effects.

4. Following the alternative ancient tradition, Lars Porsenna took Rome and abolished the monarchy before retiring after Aricia.

5. In the end, though, the evidence is just too unreliable to be sure about what happened in detail.

II. The young Republic began developing its form of government.

A. The form of Roman Republican government evolved over the centuries. The early years are, unsurprisingly, somewhat unclear.

1. Kings were replaced by two magistrates, called consuls (or *praetors*).

2. Later consular lists *(fasti)* went all the way back to 509 B.C., but there are some suspicions that the very early names are later interpolations.

3. From the early Republic the consuls shared power with colleagues with limited tenure (yearly elections).

4. There were two popular assemblies (*comitia curiata* and *comitia centuriata*).

5. In times of great emergency, a *dictator* could be installed for six months to deal with the emergency. The dictator nominated a second-in-command, the Master of Horse (*magister equitum*).

6. The former king's duties now devolved to the magistrates and to priests, the most important of whom

was the *pontifex maximus*; there was also a *rex sacrorum*, probably a purely religious incarnation of the old king.

III. The Order of the plebs may have arisen in the Early Republic.

    A. The plebeians were the other major Order of citizens.

        1. In later years, the plebs comprised all those who were not patricians.

        2. Initially, however, the plebeians may have been a restricted Order of citizens, perhaps poorer and less influential men with their own sociopolitical agenda.

        3. Rich families only appear to have joined the plebs later when the plebeians became a political and social force to be reckoned with, in the context of the Struggle of the Orders.

Essential Reading:

Livy, *Early History of Rome*, book 2.

T. J. Cornell, *The Beginnings of Rome*, chapter 9.

Supplemental Reading:

A. Alföld1, *Early Rome and the Latins*.

R. M. Ogilvie, *Early Rome and the Etruscans*, chapters 7–8.

Questions to Consider:

1. What weight, if any, can we give to the stories of the Roman Republic's foundation?

2. On what principles was power-sharing in the early Roman Republic based?

Lecture Seven—Transcript
The Beginnings of the Republic

Welcome once more to The History of Ancient Rome. We are continuing in our examination of early Roman history, and we are going to move away today from the Regal Period which has occupied our attention for the previous two lectures, and look at the foundation of the republic, the Roman Republic, established by tradition in 509 B.C., which continued as a form of government to 31 B.C. It was a long period of existence by the Roman Republic. It was a very interesting and dynamic period of history and will be the framework for our lectures for quite a while yet. It is in this period that the Romans gained control over Italy. It is in this period that they gained control over the rest of the Mediterranean, and then, toward the end of the republic, we find a fascinating process of disillusion. It is awesome to watch this happen, the unraveling of so carefully constructed system of government on the rocks of political ambition and lack of consensus. All of that is the subject for future lectures.

What I want to do today is focus on the foundation of the Republic, the transition from monarchy to republic. First we will look at the Roman traditions. I believe they are the starting point, and we should always take them into account first and foremost. We look at the Roman traditions concerning the fall of the monarchy, the expulsion of the Tarquins from Rome in 509 B.C. We will see that, unsurprisingly, these turn out to be very moralistic tales. They are very colorful, but nonetheless, the issue of historicity will be discussed as well, and we will see how, in the Roman tradition, the early republic faced some immediate challenges which it overcame by having all kinds of wonderful characters who had the right moral fiber to stand up against these challenges, meet them, and bring the republic into a new dawn.

We will also look at the shape of the early republic in its broadest outlines. These again, remain matters of tremendous uncertainty given our source material, but the broader lines have been generally agreed upon by most scholars, at least the lines of the system of government, and we will end with a discussion of the emergence of the order of plebs, the plebeians, and set the stage thereby for the discussion of the struggle of the orders in the next lecture.

In Roman tradition, the expulsion of the Tarquins, the end of monarchic government at Rome, was a very personal event. It centered around a single crime which, if you believe the sources, so incensed the Roman aristocracy that they figured they had enough not only of Tarquin, but of the whole institution of kingship, which had gone sour. The crime was committed on a woman of noble birth, Lucretia, the wife of a nobleman, Colatinus, who, with his young Turk friends was out besieging a neighboring city of the Romans, at the time. At a drinking party with his friends, the issue arose as to the relative merits of their wives, as can happen at all male drinking parties. Various men began to boast about the qualities of their wives, and Colatinus especially praised the virtue of his wife Lucretia. They decided that the best way to see if this was true was to test it. So, drunk though they were, they got on their horses (presumably there were no regulations against drunk riding in those days) and they galloped back to Rome, visited each of the houses in turn, and found many of the wives involved in parties, which is what wives are not supposed to do when their husbands are besieging neighboring towns. When they went into Lucretia's house, there she was, spinning wool with her maids.

One of the members of this party was none other than Sextus Tarquinius, the son of Tarquin the Arrogant. We are told Sextus Tarquinius was overcome with an unnatural lust for the virtuous Lucretia. At some later date, when Colatinus was away, Sextus comes back to the house of Lucretia, is invited in, invited to stay the night, and in the midst of the night, enters her bedroom, threatens her with a sword, and rapes her. He says that if she says anything, he will murder a slave and let it be known that she was raped by a slave, which he found—this act—in progress and killed the slave. He would present himself as a hero who saved Lucretia, but she would be forever humiliated by having been raped by a slave, herself and her family.

When her father and husband came back, Lucretia, unable to hide this dreadful act broke down in tears and revealed what happened. She was inconsolable, and try though they might, her men folk could not make her see the fact that she was a victim. To preserve her honor and the honor of her family, she committed suicide. One member of the group who found Lucretia, a friend of the family named Lucius Junius Brutus, a man of the nobility who was so incensed by this act, this final crime on the part of the Tarquin dynasty, that he helped rouse opinion against the Tarquins among the aristocracy, and they were thrown out of Rome. They weren't killed, but they were driven away. The republic was declared with Brutus and Colatinus as the first annual magistrates of the republic. That is the tale as we have it in our sources. It is a tale of personal transgression, with political consequences.

The saga is not over then. Tarquinius is out of Rome, but he is still alive. The first threat to the republic is a plot from inside Rome to restore the monarchy. The plot is discovered, and the leaders of the plot executed. Tarquin himself, however, is outside Rome marshaling support among his friends, among the Etruscans originally, and he makes two attempts with Etruscan backing to retake the city by violence and both attempts are defeated. The second attempt is the most threatening and is led by the king of the Etruscan town Clusium, a man with the name Lars Porsenna, an ally of Tarquin. This attempt came close to success but ultimately failed. Tarquin was not finished. He made one last attempt to rouse Rome's Latin subjects against her and attempted to seize control of Rome through rebellion among the Latins. That finally failed in 499 B.C. at the crucial battle of Lake Regillus. As a result, Tarquin gave up and retired to the Campanian town of Cumae where he died in exile.

The story is the expulsion of the Tarquins for reasons of personal crime, but then attempted retaking of the city is all very dramatic and heroic. All throughout the stories laced with wonderful romantic tales. I'll take just one example. When I was a schoolboy way back in the B.C. years, the *Lays of Ancient Rome* by Lord Macaulay was required learning in English class. This is apparently no longer in print—a shame because they are tremendous poems. There was always an image that has stuck in my head ever since, and is derived from the tales of early Rome as written by Livy, that is the story of Horatius on the bridge. The story goes that in Tarquin's second attempt to take Rome with the backing of Lars Porsenna, the Etruscan hoard came over the hill and frightened the Roman force that was across the Tiber waiting for them to approach, and the force broke up in panic. The leader of the force, a man called Horatius Cocles, organized his men, rallied them and said, "You go at the bridge." It was a wooden bridge, a bridge built by Ancus Marcius, over the Tiber. "You break up the bridge, and I will take care of the Etruscans." He single-handedly holds off the Etruscan army while his men behind hack at the bridge with their axes. Not only that, but he taunts the Etruscans as he is fighting them, away from the bridge. He mocks them and says they are the slaves of a tyrant who, with no liberty of their own, have come to rob others of their liberty, mockingly hacking them down left and right. Livy has a wonderful expression in a surge of blood to the head. Livy in a patriotic burst describes Horatius as "that great soldier whom the fortune of Rome gave to be her shield on that day of peril." Rousing stuff. You want to go out and beat up some Etruscans. The bridge finally collapses behind Horatius and he is left stranded facing his enemies. So, he jumps into the Tiber River fully armed and swims across where he is met with tremendous hullabaloo, multiple honors are bestowed upon him and a public statue is erected in his honor.

What do we have? We have more moral tales. We have tales of moral fiber. After all, Livy in his introduction to his history states, unequivocally, that the function of his description of Roman history is to present *exempla*, models of behavior, good and bad. His other main function is to trumpet the Roman achievement and the glories of the Roman nation. He states that quite clearly in Book One in his preface to his history. Here is why I am doing this. I want to present examples. In the cycle of tales around the expulsion of the Tarquins there are wonderful examples of that. We have Lucretia, that paradigm of womanly virtue. She is so concerned about her own honor and the honor of her family—and by that I mean her family's men folk and their name—that she commits suicide rather than face the disgrace of being accused of having been raped by a slave or having been raped at all, even if they could prove Tarquin to have been the perpetrator. We have the martial model of Horatius Cocles, patriot and gallant warrior who single-handedly holds off the Etruscan army and risks his own life to save the state.

That is a great model of martial prowess. We have in the first council Lucius Junius Brutus, the man considered generally to have been the founder of the republic since he organized the coup d'état that ousted the Tarquins. We have in him another, rather more difficult for us in the modern world to understand, but a model of what the Romans considered a most admirable quality, the quality of *severitas*, the quality of sticking by your principles regardless of how hard it might be. This centers on what I mentioned earlier, the attempted restoration of the monarchy from within Rome. What I did not say was that the leaders of that attempted restoration were the sons of Brutus. Brutus as the magistrate had to preside over the execution of his own sons, which he did. We might find that somewhat disturbing, but for the Romans this is a model of *severitas*, standing firm beside your principles, which are the principles now of liberty and freedom in the face of anarchic oppression, even if it means executing your own children.

Moral tales. What do we do with these moral tales? Modern scholars have come up with various explanations. For those who believe in the wider Etruscan control of central Italy, then naturally enough, the expulsion of the Tarquins fits into the waning power of the Etruscans in central Italy. Enough of that—I don't need to go into that any more. There are others who take a rather more extreme view. They dismiss completely the legends and moral tales surrounding the expulsion of the kings and say, "What we have going on is not a single catastrophic revolutionary event, unlike the expulsion of the Tarquins. Rather, it is a process of evolution." What we have is a gradual process of the devolution of the kings power to annual magistrates. Eventually, the king is sort of phased out of the picture. This process is going on for maybe 70 or 80 years. Some of them argue that it goes down maybe to 450 B.C. So it is a long process of evolution that is basically being ignored completely by the Roman sources and presented as this single event surrounded by all these wonderful romantic tales. That view doesn't carry much weight among the majority of scholars. It is considered to be too extreme.

Another view is to see in the story of Lucretia events that are not entirely improbable. This approach would say that within royal dynasties, personal acts could actually have tremendous political consequences. It is not unlikely that a transgression of that nature by a prince against a nobleman's wife might have severe political ramifications for the dynasty as a whole. They would point to other well-documented dynasties for those of you perhaps who have seen or heard professor Jeremy McInerney's course on Ancient Greece, you may be familiar with the stories of the expulsion of the tyrants from Greece, the tyrant Hippias is driven out of Athens over a lovers quarrel between himself, his brother and three other men. Here is an event that has a personal quality but severe political ramifications for the tyranny at Athens. So, similarly goes the argument, it is quite possible that something like this actually took place and that it was a personal event that led to the Tarquins expulsion.

The view that I find the most intriguing is one that peeks through now and then from the ancient sources, an alternative tradition about the monarchy. That tradition, which is mentioned in a few Roman sources, records that Lars Porsenna, the Etruscan king of Clusium, captured Rome. He actually took it. Then, he presumably abolished the monarchy. Why he did so is not clear. All we get are vague hints that this took place. In the end it has to be said that the evidence we have is not sufficiently clear for us to make a definite determination among these competing possibilities. Once again, we have competing possibilities.

Whatever the case, when the Tarquins were expelled, the fledgling republic began to adopt its distinctive shape, and it is worth looking at that. As we will see, the Roman Republic, during its long period of existence went through a very protracted process of evolution in terms of its polity, in terms of the shape of its government. Naturally enough, the very earliest phases of it are somewhat unclear, but the broad outline seems to be generally agreed upon by most scholars in the field. Essentially, the kings are replaced by two annually elected magistrates who are called *consuls* or possibly *praetors*. The latter phrase *praetors* seems to be a form of magistry that is found within the Etruscan cities. It may be that the Romans adopted that term first to indicate these two annually elected magistrates. You have two men. As I mentioned at the start, the first two are Junius Brutus and Colatinus. Then, every year, there are new elections, and they are replaced. I am going to call them consuls for the sake of clarity. Just to let you know, one of the examples of the uncertainty of this early period is that we are not even really clear about what these guys are called at the start, either consuls or *praetors*.

What is noteworthy about this system of government is that two basic principles that were to forever mark office holding in republican Rome are established at the very outset. You have a limited tenure of office of one year's duration, and you always have at least one other colleague, one other person with the same powers as yourself holding that office. Collegiality, having at least one colleague, and only holding the office for a limited period (tenure), these two principles, if we believe our sources, were established right at the start. There is no reason to disbelieve it. Comparative data from Greece would suggest that this is quite common, kings being replaced by annual magistrates. How do we know who the consuls were? The Romans kept a list of them. They are called *fasti*, and they are a matter of considerable debate and uncertainty. The *fasti* are lists, year by year, of who the consuls were. They seem to go right back to the very start, back to 509 B.C. There are two views on the believability of the *fasti*, the skeptical view and the more trusting view. The skeptical view is that the *fasti* have suffered, especially the earliest years of it, from about 280 B.C., have suffered from interpolation from later periods.

Skeptics point out that you have families that are in better documented times prominent among the listed consuls, have nothing going back for centuries, and then suddenly, one of them appears in the very earliest lists. They say this is clearly a case of later families sticking their names into the past to get themselves better historical credentials. The more trusting people take the diametrically opposite view from the same evidence. This is what is so fascinating about this, I find, and so typical of ancient history. They point to the opposite case. They say you have consuls in the early lists with names that never appear again. Why invent people who are nobodies. Surely the names must reflect historical reality. You decide. Whatever the case, later Romans had a list of consuls so they could tell year by year who they were and it went all the way back to 509 B.C., back to the supposed start of the republic.

In addition to the consuls, we have already seen that there was the *comitia curiata* from the Regal Period, and possibly stretching back to the Regal Period, the other assembly of the people, the *comitia centuriata*, the assembly of people organized into centuries. These two popular assemblies remained and became cornerstones of the new republic. It was the *comitia centuriata*, the centurion military assembly that elected the consuls every year. The *comitia curiata* are the ones who conferred *imperium* on the consuls as they had done on the kings. If you want to think of it this way, on one day, the citizens would assemble in the centuries to hold elections for the consuls. Once the two consuls had been elected, on some other subsequent day, the same people would assemble again, this time in their *curia* to confer and ratify the choice and confer imperium on the counsels. Remember, *imperium* always comes from the Roman people. That is another key concept of the Roman Republic.

The consuls then replaced the king. They took over the main judicial and military function of the king, but the Romans were a highly practical people. They said sometimes in emergencies it is not going to be possible to have two commanders with equal power. You might have a gridlock situation at a crucial moment when a firm hand is needed. So, they allowed for a temporary monarchy. They worked into their early republic a system that allowed for, in extreme circumstances, the appointment of a man called a *dictator*. A man who spoke, and the people listened. That is the idea behind it. He was an extraordinary magistrate. He was chosen from among the members of the Senate. Precisely how in the early years is unclear. In later years, he was chosen from among the ex-consuls. He did not have a colleague. His job was to sort out the problem he had been appointed to sort out. So, he was only chosen in extraordinary circumstances and given the job "Fix that." That was his job. He appointed below him an assistant called the master of horse. The *magistor equator*, the master of the cavalry, which suggests that the original function of this office was definitely military. It was to sort out or obviate the possibility that two consuls who disagreed about how the war should be carried out would gridlock the Roman effort in that war and appoint a definite general to carry out a specific task. Once again, a dictatorship is to carry put a specific task and is appointed only in extraordinary circumstances.

In addition to the dictator, the king's religious duties devolved onto the nobility, and specifically the old preexisting college of the pontificates who were probably around from the Regal Period, and the chief of the pontifical college, the *pontifex maximus* now rose up as the chief priest of Rome. He basically took over much of the kings' duties in the religious sphere. Forever afterwards, the *pontifex maximus* was the chief priest of Rome. He is the one chiefly responsible for maintaining the good relationship with the gods. We will look in the later lecture at the system of Roman paganism, its belief system and the way that it was administered by the various officials who ran it. Suffice it to say right now that the priestly colleges were not made up of any separate entity or class from the politicians. It is the nobility who provide Rome with its politicians, its generals and its priests. They are all the same people. One can be a priest, general, and consul all at the same time. That is an important point to appreciate as well early on.

The king himself is generally agreed to have survived in vestigial form in the position of the *rex sacrorum*, the king of the sacred rights. Why this was so is unclear. Various arguments have been put forward. The relationship between the *pontiff ex maximus* and the king of sacred rights has been discussed at wont. They had to go into all those details, a very fine detail that we don't want to have to delve into. Suffice it to say that I think the majority of you are safe in thinking that the *rex sacrorum*, this king of the sacred rights is a vestige of the old king depoliticized. Unlike all the other priests, the *rex sacrorum* is not allowed to be a member of the Senate. His duties are specifically religious and he is essentially excluded from the political life of the state which I think supports the view that the *rex sacrorum* is a sort of stripped down king, the king divested of his political power but still responsible for various religious duties.

Such then is broadly speaking the roughly agreed upon shape of the early republic. So many of these issues are a matter of debate and uncertainty. I am presenting you with what I believe to be the majority view in most of these cases. We have seen in the previous lecture on Regal society the appearance of the order called the patriciate, or the patrician order—the Latin word order referring to a rank, a social status. It seems that in the early republic we have the appearance for the first time of the other order that was to become dominant in the early republic and influence the shaping of the early republic and politics of this period, and that is the plebeian order.

In our ancient sources, the plebeians are presented as always being there. They were there beside the patricians, and constituted of everybody else. All the people, at least all the freeborn citizen body who were not patricians, were classified as plebeians. It has struck certain scholars as extremely curious that they should be described as an order. Why not just call them "everyone else"? The order really implies some sort of organization or limitation on membership.

It seems to be the case; at least it has been argued forcefully, that the plebeians are a rather more restricted body of citizens who grew up in opposition to, perhaps as a foil to the patricians at some early stage. They seem to have their own socio-political agenda. So, who they were we can't say. We don't have the evidence available to us, especially since the Romans believed the plebeians were always there; it confuses the matter even more. A good case can be made that the plebeians arose in the early republic parallel to the patrician class with their own socio-political agenda. Whether or not there were rich and influential families in the plebeian order is a matter of some discussion. The case seems to be that the richer, non-patrician families of Rome joined the plebeian order later. As we will see in the next lecture, in the course of a major formative event in the early republic, what the Romans called the Struggle of the Orders, the plebeians began agitating for certain privileges, rights, reforms and changes in the way the state was run. Our evidence would suggest that initially, those first motions for agitation were of a socio-economic nature, which would apply to the lesser well-off people in Roman society. So, the argument goes that the plebeians were originally the less influential, non-patrician families, who in the course of the struggle of the orders, joined forces with richer non-patrician families to form the final plebeian order of the later era. That is a story that we should postpone to the next lecture.

Lecture Eight
The Struggle of the Orders

Scope:

In this lecture, we examine the so-called Struggle of the Orders, which was a socio-political conflict between the patricians and the plebs that dominated Roman domestic politics from 494 B.C. to 287 B.C. Despite concerns about the quality of the ancient sources for our information about these events, the outline seems clear enough. It was a protracted struggle between the Orders over social, economic, and judicial issues of interest to the plebs and over access to the political system. Its resolution lent a new shape to the government of the Republic.

Outline

I. The written sources for the Struggle of the Orders portray it simplistically, but a close reading can reveal some of the genuine issues that generated the conflict.

    A. The later sources for the Struggle, which survive for us to read, are not without problems, but they are usable nonetheless.

        1. Our sources depict the Struggle as an entirely political one, and they appear to retroject later patterns of behavior onto this early period.

        2. In fact, some of the original issues can be discerned, however dimly.

        3. Despite the problems of the evidence, then, the outline of the Struggle is clear enough, even if the details are more open to question.

    B. The issues that appear to have generated the Struggle of the Orders can be discerned.

        1. Our later sources focus on one such issue—access to the political system. This issue appears, however, to have arisen only later in the Struggle.

        2. Relief from debt and, in particular, from debt-bondage was an early issue.

        3. The plebs also demanded judicial reform and codification of the laws to prevent arbitrary treatment at the hands of aristocrats.

    4. There was a desire for reform to distribute newly conquered territories among the poorer citizens.

    5. The Struggle, then, was really a series of struggles over different issues. Our later sources have simplified this complex picture considerably.

II. The Struggle of the Orders dominated Roman politics in the early Republic.

  A. The patricians dominated the Roman political system in the early Republic.

    1. Plebs were not excluded *per se*, as the consular lists *(fasti)* show.

    2. At some stage in the mid-fifth century the patriciate "closed" and no additional families were admitted to its ranks. The closed patriciate then dominated politics.

    3. One thread of conflict in the Struggle was to "re-open" access to the political system to non-patricians.

    4. But even before the "closing" of the patriciate there were signs of trouble.

  B. In 494 B.C. the plebs "seceded" from Rome, since their demands for economic and social reform were not met.

    1. The plebs demanded release from debt, particularly debt-bondage and arbitrary treatment at the hands of aristocrats. This suggests that the plebs were originally comprised of the poorer elements in society.

    2. They left Rome and formed their own, parallel state on the Janiculum, a nearby hill.

    3. The "Plebeian State" was modeled on the main, patrician-dominated Republic: it had a council (the *concilium plebis*); it had elected officers (tribunes of the plebs and *aediles* of the plebs); it passed resolutions called *plebiscita*.

    4. The plebs were now firmly established as a force in Roman politics.

    5. Exactly how the First Secession was brought to an end is unclear from our sources.

  C. Subsequent secessions of the plebs forced further reform.

    1. A crisis in 451–449 revolved around the plebs' demand for codification of the laws.

2. A Committee of Ten *(decemviri)* was established to draw up a law code, but it attempted to subvert the Republic and rule as a junta. The head of the Committee was Appius Claudius.
3. In response, the plebs seceded, the Committee of Ten was ousted, and Rome got its first code of written law, the Twelve Tables, in 449 B.C.
4. As a result, the Plebeian State earned recognition from the Republic and was assimilated into it.
5. Plebeian demands for land, debt relief, and political equality continued in the ensuing decades, and the plebs were partially successful in having them met.
6. By 367 B.C. the main part of the Struggle of the Orders was over, but the epilogue came only in 287 B.C. when a law (the *Lex Hortensia*) made *plebiscita* binding on all citizens, patrician and plebeian.

III. The Struggle of the Orders helped shape the form of the developed Republican government in Rome; it also had important social effects.

A. In the evolution of the Roman Republican government, the Struggle of the Orders stands out as the major formative influence.

B. In the last phases of the Struggle, the Plebeian State came to be assimilated with the Republic.

C. New magistracies were created to suit both plebeian and patrician.
1. One consul a year was to be plebeian.
2. *Curule* (patrician) *aediles* were created to match *aediles* of the plebs.
3. A new magistracy, the *praetorship*, was open to both Orders.

D. The nature of the Roman ruling class was also transformed by the Struggle.
1. With the closing of the patriciate in ca. 450 B.C., wealthy non-patricians joined forces with the plebs.
2. This transformed the plebeian movement into a socially diverse entity with differing goals: the rich plebs wanted access to the political system, the poorer ones wanted socioeconomic reforms.

3. The resolution of the Struggle and the admission of the plebs into the political system created a patrician-plebeian ruling class that was largely unconcerned by the demands of the commoners for reform.

4. After 287 B.C. the patrician/plebeian distinction became more socially than politically significant. New lines of stratification began to emerge, but they were tied to Roman imperial expansion.

Essential Reading:

Livy, *Early History of Rome*, books 2–3.

T. J. Cornell, *The Beginnings of Rome*, chapters 10, 11, 13.

Supplemental Reading:

R. M. Ogilvie, *Early Rome and the Etruscans*, chapters 8–11.

Questions to Consider:

1. How reliable are our sources for the Struggle of the Orders?

2. To what degree were the original goals of the Struggle "subverted" by the selfish demands of the non-patrician upper classes for access to government?

Lecture Eight—Transcript
The Struggle of the Orders

Hello and welcome back to The History of Ancient Rome, Lecture Eight in the series. The last time, we examined the foundation of the Roman Republic, and we saw that the problems of evidence that dog the investigation of Roman history are unabated for that particular issue. Things don't get much better when we come to look at the early republic, which continues in our sources to contain stories that are clearly models of ethical moral behavior, rather than historical accounts of events. One thing does shine through from the evidence, and that is a socio-political conflict that started very early in the republic's history and continued for the best part of two centuries on and off and was considered by the Romans to have shaped their republic in a decisive way.

That struggle is referred to as the Struggle of the Orders, or the Conflict of the Orders, and refers to an ongoing debate and conflict between the patricians and the plebeians over numerous issues. What I want to do today in our lecture is to examine the broad outline of the struggle, see how it is presented to us in the ancient authors we have available to us, try to reconstruct what actually was going on in the background, there are hints in the sources that something more complicated than they portray was in progress, then look at the resolution of the conflict and its ramifications for later Roman history.

In our sources, the Struggle of the Orders is presented overwhelmingly as a political struggle over access to the higher offices of the Roman state and the political system of the Roman Republic. Many scholars find this very suspicious since the course of the Struggle in our sources seems to reflect very closely the course of better documented and later conflict in the Roman republic which later was to bring about the collapse of the republic and is referred to by modern scholars as the Roman Revolution. The process started in 133 B.C. and continues down to 31 B.C. That is a process we will be giving attention to in due course, but many scholars find it suspicious that the Struggle of the Orders looks so much like the Roman Revolution. What they conclude from this is that the later authors have retrojected a familiar pattern of conflict back into the distant ill-documented past. Other scholars argue differently and say the rather restricted scope of political conflict and discourse in ancient Roman society probably means that they argued over much the same thing whether in 400 B.C. or in 100 B.C. Whether or not you adhere to one view or another is a matter of how you approach the evidence. It is cause for some suspicion to see that the Struggle of the Orders is presented to us as a sort of earlier version of the Roman Revolution.

Our sources present this as a relatively straightforward dispute over access to the higher offices of the state between the plebeians and patricians. They portray the patricians as dominating the consulship and the plebeians as agitating continuously to get in on the consulship and the upper offices of state, eventually being admitted. There are some hints in our sources that the Struggle of the Orders ran deeper than this, and it is on those deeper issues that I would like to turn our attention now.

In addition to access to the political system, as I say the dominant theme comes through from written evidence, we also hear that the plebs were demanding relief from debt. This was specifically a form of debt that is known as debt bondage. Debt bondage is a rather complex procedure. It is not that you go to your bank manager, ask for a chariot loan, and then, when you fail to pay become a slave. Debt bondage is actually a means used in archaic societies, usually one that lacks masses of slave labor, to acquire for the upper classes cheap labor by provision of subsistence to poor or destitute people in return for their work. The work is normally proscribed as a form of servitude, slavery. It seems that it can be abused. Once you find yourself in debt bondage, it can be very difficult to get out because you are in a spiral of being dependent on someone who is supplying you with your subsistence and for whom you have to continually work in order to survive. One could find oneself quickly as a full-blown slave, even though you are technically a sort of indentured servant. As a result, debt bondage was something that would definitely have effected the lower orders of society. If you had a bad crop and needed subsistence, you could find yourself caught in the cycle of debt bondage and obligated to a rich or more influential person. This was something that the plebs were agitating for reform.

They also appeared to have been agitating for judicial reform in the form of some codification of the laws. We have seen how in the Regal Period, the king was the font of all law. In the absence of the king, it was the chief magistrates of the state who now became the font of all law. They are the ones who decided on judicial matters.

Apparently, their treatment of the lower orders could be arbitrary. As a result, the plebs were agitating for a codification of the law, some reform of the written and agreed upon law that applies to everyone equally so that people would know their rights and know their positions on certain issues when they came before a magistrate. Again, this is another issue that would seem to affect the lower orders rather than the upper orders. There also seems to have been a demand for the distribution of land from the newly conquered territories. We will be turning our attention in the next lecture to the expansion of Rome in Italy. As Roman power expanded, more and more land came into the orbit of the Roman state, and there was a demand from the plebs that this land be distributed evenly and that the upper classes don't just grab everything for themselves.

Really, what we are talking about is not so much a Struggle of the Orders, but the Struggles of the Orders over a variety of different issues. The earliest ones appear to have been the socio-economic issues of debt-bondage and release from debt, later land distribution and access to the political system. So, it is a much more complicated picture than our sources tend to present. They do present hints of these other aspects of the struggle at various points in their accounts.

It must be stated that we don't have a consistent account of the Struggle of the Orders, rather a series of snippets of information, vignettes if you like, references to it and so forth which makes working on it difficult indeed. The early republic was dominated by the patricians. The notion that the patricians had always dominated the state doesn't seem to be true. If we turn to the *fasti*, the annual list of consuls, we can see that in the period from the foundation of the republic, if we start at 509 B.C., and take the story down to about 400 B.C. or so, we can see that in that period at the start, plebeians were given access to the higher offices of the state, but that gradually in the course of the fifth century, their access to that system was closed off. This pattern of office holding was often called the Closing of the Patricia. This was the time when the patricians ceased to accept new members into their order and started to tend to monopolize the higher offices of state, giving rise to the demand for access to the political system. It can be noted from the percentages of office holding by patricians and by plebeians over this time that the closing of the Patricia only becomes really pronounced in the middle of the fifth century B.C. Therefore, the demand for access to the political system seems to have come into the struggle of the orders later, as a secondary issue. We hear from our sources that prior to 450 B.C. there were already signs of trouble in the state. The issues agitating the pleb must have been issues other than access to the political system, since they had not been shut out of the upper offices at that early stage.

The first real event in the Struggle of the Orders that we hear about takes place in 494 B.C. In this year, we hear that the plebs demanded relief from debt and debt bondage, which they were finding oppressive. They also wanted some relief from arbitrary treatment at the hands of the aristocrats. This would tend to suggest that the plebs were originally constituted of the socially and economically depressed elements in society. When their demands were not met, they resorted to a very interesting ploy: they seceded from Rome. They walked out the gates over to a hill, the Janiculum, and left the city empty. This is how it is portrayed. Suddenly, we have patricians sitting around in Rome, and there are no plebeians to treat arbitrarily or to subject to bondage. Whether they did that, whether they actually physically left the city and abandoned it, seems most unlikely since Rome was at war with various neighbors at this time, and those neighbors would have taken tremendous advantage of the complete absence of the rank and file of the Roman army, but that some sort of civic protest took place would seem to be what the secession was actually about.

In any case, our traditions record that they left the city and set up shop on the Janiculum Hill where they established a parallel state. We call it the Plebeian State, which they modeled on the patrician republic in the following way. We have seen that in the republic, there were two popular assemblies organized on centuries (military units that was called the centurion assembly) and an assembly organized around *curia* (another grouping of citizens that is most unclear to us). Just like this, the plebeians set up their own assembly, which they called the Council of the Plebs, the *concilian plebus*. Only plebs were allowed, of course. So, they set up a parallel to the popular assemblies. They organized this, it seems, along the tribal lines, the divisions of people into local units of tribes. That is certainly how it was organized later. Whether it was organized that way at its inception is a different matter. That is how it was organized in later years.

So, as you have voting blocks in the republic's *comitia curiata* and *centuriata*, you have voting blocks in the Council of the Plebs. Just as the republic had its magistrates, the two annually elected consuls, so too the plebs have their own officers, which are called *tribunes,* which seems to mean tribal officer since the assembly that elected them was based on tribal units. Then, the tribunes were tribal officers. They are called tribunes of the plebs. Just as there were two consuls, there were originally two tribunes. The purpose of the tribunes was to represent the interests of the plebs and defend their interests against opponents. The plebs also elected two further officers called *aediles* of the plebs. They were new things, and they first appeared in the context of the plebeian state in this early secession from Rome.

Just like the Roman Republic, the plebeians would meet in their council. They would have propositions put to them by their officers, and they would vote on those propositions. When those propositions were passed, they were called *plebescite.* These are decisions of the plebs, initially binding only on the plebs since no one else recognized them, but eventually we will see the plebeian state came to be integrated into the republic to give us a fully developed Roman Republic, Roman state.

All this is presented to us as happening in 494 B.C. It might not all have happened at this time. This may be a process of evolution. The first secession marks out the plebs as separate from the patricians. They are agitating for political, social, and judicial justice. Then they start to organize themselves into this parallel state. It might have been a gradual process. It might not have happened in the summer of 494, but whatever the case, in the course of the early fifth century, a plebeian state emerges parallel to the Patrician dominated republic.

Exactly how the situation was resolved in 494 B.C. and the years following is its unclear from our sources, so we will have to leave that situation sit. The agitation continued, however. The Struggle of the Orders did not end, and the next real benchmark of the Struggle of the Orders takes place in the mid-fifth century B.C. in the years between 451 B.C. and 449 B.C., which also marks a hallmark in Roman legal history. In this time, the plebeian demands for codification of the law were ongoing. It was decided in a rather wonderful tradition, that they would send an emissary to Athens to find out how the Greeks had codified their laws under their great leader Solon, years before. Armed with these wonderful plans and ideas, this embassy came back, and it was decided in 451 B.C. that a board of ten men would be established to codify the laws of the state. For reasons that are completely unclear, it was also decided that while this board was in power, the regular constitution of the government would be suspended. There would be no consuls. There would just be this board of ten to codify the laws.

Headed by one of the earliest personalities we can grasp from Roman history, a man called Appius Claudius, the board sets about its job and produces ten tables (tablets) that were put up in public of laws in 451 B.C. It seems that the agitation for further reform continued. So, it was decided that the board of ten should continue into the next year. The board was reelected, Appius Claudius again at its head, but something went terribly wrong in the second year of the board's tenure of office. They became a junta of sorts that tried to take over the state. They went around behaving arbitrarily, making judicial decisions against people without any justification, marching around with all the symbols of power (*imperium*) even though they weren't entitled to them, and so on, until it became known as the Ten Tarquins. They published two more tables of law bringing the total to twelve, and then refused to step down from power. In this crisis, the plebs seceded a second time. They simply left and said if you want to rule a city, rule and empty one. They departed a second time and forced the Ten Tarquins to step down. Appius Claudius was imprisoned and committed suicide before facing trial for his crimes.

The result of this process was that the plebeian state was recognized by the republic. In many ways, the action of the plebs had saved the state from tyranny. Whatever about the original status of the plebeian state vis-à-vis the republic, by 450 it was recognized and came to be folded in to the republic in a certain way.

The Struggle of the Orders continued because there were still certain demands for relief from debt, land distribution and so forth. Now, at this stage, the *patriciate* had closed; rich, non-patrician families allied themselves with what was a very effective political tool in the state, the Plebeian Order. They changed the face of the Plebeian Order and began agitating for access to the political system. Without going into the details of it (most of the details are most unclear to us) by 367 B.C., many of the social and economic problems that faced the Struggle of the Orders had been resolved. A series of laws were passed in this year 367 B.C., that ended much of the Struggle's political aspect. At this time it was decided that one of the consuls every year had to be a plebeian. It was mandated by law that the plebeians had access to the political system. In addition, in full recognition of the political state, the patricians created their own parallels to the plebeian officers. They did not create tribunes, but they created two more *aediles* who were to be only patricians. Now you have four *aediles* a year. Two will be *curule aediles* (patricians), because they sit in a certain kind of chair called a *curule* chair (ivory inlaid chair) apparently an Etruscan style of chair that was used as the Etruscan throne. Only patricians could use such a chair when sitting in office, and then two plebeian *aediles*.

In addition, a new magistracy was created, the *praetorship* to be one step below the consulship. This new magistracy was to be open to both orders equally. So, The Struggle of the Orders in its essence ended by 367 B.C., and sees at the end the inclusions of the plebeians, the folding of the plebeian state into the patrician republic to form what is essentially the Roman Republic that we all know and love from later years, which we will be looking at in more detail later in this course. As a postscript to—there is one point I want to make before moving on to that. It should be noted that there was one consul a year that was mandated to be plebeian. The inverse was not the case. It was not mandated that one consul a year had to be patrician. So, it was possible to have two plebeian consuls, impossible to have two patrician counsels.

A postscript to the Struggle of the Orders comes in 287 B.C. Up to this time, as we have seen, despite the recognition of the plebeian state by the patrician dominated republic, the *plebiscites* of the plebs seem to have been binding only in themselves. There is some discussion. How do they enforce their decisions? How does the Council of the Plebs enforce its resolutions? It would seem to be through the threat of civil disobedience. If people refuse to accept their decisions, they could always secede, or refuse to cooperate with whatever order had been issued to them. If they were in any way challenged, they could call on their tribunes, their officers to help them. This is an extremely confrontational mode of doing things, but in 287 B.C. it was clear that this was no longer going to work. So, a law was passed which mandated that the decisions of the plebs, the *plebiscites*, were binding on all citizens. In other words, the *plebiscites* gained the force of the law. This was to have very important constitutional ramifications in the Roman state. What it meant was that the Council of the Plebs was now a legislative body of the state. It could pass essentially laws that were applicable to all people in the state.

I should point out that the twelve tables that were instituted in 451 and 450 B.C. no longer survive. They are the first body of Roman law. They have not survived intact, but they have survived in fragments, in quotations in later authors, since these were basic texts that all Roman schoolboys learned by heart when they were in school. They have been reconstructed. People will say, "as the law in Table One says," so scholars have put them all together and come up with at least a partial reconstruction of the Twelve Tables of Roman Law, and they are a fascinating document. They are one of our earliest documents on Roman history. They date to the fifth century B.C., and they tell us that a lot of the features of Roman society that the Romans considered to be very old were indeed extremely old. In the Twelve Tables, we find mentions of slavery and debt bondage. We find mention of patricians and plebeians. These obviously go back at least into the fifth century. We find also a mention of patrons and clients, another key feature of Roman society. This also is a feature of the society that the Twelve Tables were written for.

That the tables as cited in these authors are valid, and not just inventions of later ages, is suggested by the very archaic nature of the Latin used in these quotations. When an author cites, "as table X says, (about this particular subject," then quotes a table it will be in a very old fashioned style of Latin, one that would not be current at the time the author was writing and this suggests that these citations are actually from Twelve Tables of law that were put up in the fifth century, and allow us to see that we are not completely off the mark. It is nice to have a check in the sea of uncertainty for the written sources, it is nice to have a check to see that we are not completely off the mark as we reconstruct the broad shape of these early conflicts in the Roman Republic and the shape of society as a whole.

The Struggle of the Orders was largely completed by 367 B.C., but definitely nailed into its coffin by 287 B.C. with *lex hortensia,* the law that mandated that the *plebiscites* be binding on all citizens. This decision had enormous effects on the Roman state. It changed the way things were done in the Roman state. It introduced new elements into the Roman governmental system, the elements of the Council of the Plebs, the tribunes of the plebs, *aediles,* and *plebiscites.* All these are originally separatist, are secessionist patterns of behavior by the plebs came to be folded into the republic and became part and parcel of doing things in the Roman state. That was to have enormous ramifications in the Roman Revolution.

With the closing of the *patriciate* and the access gained by the rich, non-patrician, plebeian families, into the upper echelon of the state with the laws of 367 B.C., the nature of the Roman ruling class was also transformed. If the plebeians had started out as the lower orders of society agitating for social, economic and judicial justice, when they were joined by the rich upper class non-patrician elements, they were transformed. The plebeians themselves were transformed. When the rich plebs got what they wanted which was access to the political system, they melded with the patricians to form what is often called the patrician/plebeian ruling class. (Roman historians don't have a tremendous amount of imagination.) The joint ruling class of the later Roman state is often called the patrician/plebeian ruling class. What this meant was that the upper orders now looked to their own interests, and the rich plebeians tended to disregard the agitation from the lower orders. They got what they wanted. What they wanted was a slice of the cake, and they had been given that slice. Now, whether or not debt bondage was a problem, or there was widespread debt, the distribution of land and so forth, those issues no longer concerned them, because they were in the club of ruling the state. This was also to have severe ramifications for the future. Many of the issues that had agitated the plebs in the first place were not addressed, although in 326 B.C. debt bondage was abolished. Debt wasn't. Debt and land distribution continued to be burning issues for the lower orders of the Roman state and were to reappear in the Roman Revolution as serious stimuli to action.

With the melding of the plebeians and patricians into a single ruling order, the nature of the Roman elite also changed. The distinction between plebeian and patrician became far less important politically. It was still a socially powerful division. Remember one was patrician by name. As a result, you could have some cachet by your name. The distinction was no longer important politically. Pretty much the running of the state was open to both patricians and plebeians. What became more important now was relative wealth. The new Roman nobility came to be formulated around relative wealth, concepts of plutocracy in many ways. All wealthy citizens whether patricians or plebeians could stand for the offices of state and the consulship. So, the patrician/ plebeian division recedes as an important political entity in the wake of the law of 287 B.C., and a new Roman nobility is what emerges to rule the empire, which, over the whole time that I have been talking today was an ongoing endeavor. It is to the rise of Roman power in Italy that we turn our attention in the next lecture.

Lecture Nine
Roman Expansion in Italy

Scope:

The Roman conquest of Italy, effected between the eighth and third centuries B.C., was a long and arduous business. In this lecture we chart the outline of this expansion in three phases, which were not without their major reverses for the Romans. We close by examining the ramifications of Roman expansion for Roman politics and society.

Outline

I. For the first four centuries of its existence, Rome was occupied with gaining control over Latium.

    A. The early dealings of Rome with its Latin neighbors are shrouded in obscurity, but they appear varied and complex.

        1. The sources for the early expansion of Rome are not good. They are full of heroic and patriotic tales that served as models for good behavior in later generations. From the Third Samnite War onwards, however, our material improves considerably.

        2. The sources depict the kings mixing war and diplomacy in their dealings with the Latins.

        3. The transition from the monarchy to the Republic weakened the Roman position (see Lars Porsenna), but victory over the Latins at the Battle of Lake Regillus in 499 B.C. recovered the situation.

        4. The Treaty of Cassius (*foedus Cassianum*) in 493 B.C. established a new relationship between Rome and the Latins, who were formed into the so-called Latin League.

        5. The outline of the Treaty seems clear, but the details are not.

            a. It was a military alliance (non-aggression pact; mutual friends and enemies; equal division of spoils of war).

            b. Romans were to command any joint forces.

            c. It is unclear whether Rome was a member of the Latin League or whether the Treaty was a bilateral agreement between Rome and the League.

B. The requirements of defense against tribal mountain peoples in the neighborhood of Latium strengthened Rome's position among the Latins.

    1. The Aequi and Volsci, tribal mountain-dwellers, launched annual raids into Latium between ca. 500 and 440 B.C. Rome and the Latins resisted in tandem.

    2. The continuous warfare strengthened Roman influence over the Latins.

C. Incursions into Etruria brought Rome and the Latins close to war when disaster struck from the north. Roman recovery led to the final conquest of Latium.

    1. In the course of the fifth century, Rome had begun a series of conflicts with Veii, a powerful Etruscan town north of the Tiber.

    2. In 396 the Romans captured Veii and took all the spoils for themselves.

    3. As the Latins were about to fight over their treatment by the Romans, disaster struck from the north.

    4. Gallic raiders from the Po Valley region, known as Gallia Cisalpina, defeated a combined Roman/Latin force at Allia in 390 B.C. and captured Rome. The Romans paid the Gauls off and they left.

    5. The Gallic raid humiliated the Romans but does not seem to have greatly undermined their overall position.

    6. Roman incursions into Etruria and Latium continued until 338 B.C., when the Romans defeated a combined Latin force and reshaped the Latin League to their own needs.

II. The Samnite Wars were on a larger scale than any previously fought by Rome, and Roman victory in the conflicts secured Roman power over all of central Italy.

A. The Samnites were formidable opponents.

    1. The Samnites were a federation of tribal people living in the mountains of central Italy.

    2. Tough fighting men, they were a warrior society that prized martial skill.

    3. Initially, they made a non-aggression pact with Rome.

    4. Samnite raids into Campania caused the inhabitants to appeal to Rome for help in 343 B.C.

5. The First Samnite War (343–41 B.C.) ended with renewal of the Romano-Samnite Treaty.

B. The encroachment of Roman power on Samnite borders caused the Second Samnite War, an epic struggle that lasted more than twenty years.
   1. The Romans continued to extend their influence into the outlying regions of Samnium.
   2. War broke out in 326 and lasted until 304 B.C.
   3. It was a great struggle that tested Roman resolve in the face of catastrophes such as the Caudine Forks in 321 B.C.
   4. By a combination of military operations and diplomacy, the Romans encircled the Samnites in their mountain homeland and forced their surrender.
   5. The old Romano-Samnite Treaty was renewed, but Roman power now extended deep into former Samnite territory.

C. The conflict called the Third Samnite War (298–290) was, in fact, the last stand of free Italy in the face of Roman expansion. The Romans' victory gave them complete control over central Italy.
   1. With the end of the Second Samnite War, free Italians could have no illusions about what the Romans were ultimately aiming for.
   2. Although sparked by Roman assistance to people attacked by the Samnites, the Third Samnite War became a pan-Italic stand against Roman expansion.
   3. A coalition of Samnites, Umbrians, Etruscans and Gauls fought the Romans at Sentinum in 295 B.C., the largest battle yet fought on Italian soil.
   4. The Roman victory led to the incorporation of the Samnites into the Roman administration of Italy in 290 B.C.
   5. The Romans were now dominant in central Italy, although some mopping-up operations continued for several decades.

III. Conflict with the Greek colony of Tarentum led to the invasion of Pyrrhus, Rome's first overseas enemy.

A. Tarentum, pressed by Roman expansion, called upon King Pyrrhus of Epirus for help.

B. Tarentum found itself facing Roman power in the 280s B.C.

C. In conflict with Rome, the Tarentines called upon Pyrrhus of Epirus, who invaded Italy in 281 B.C. with an army of 25,000 men and 20 elephants.

D. Commanding a well-trained and well-equipped army fighting in the formidable Macedonian phalanx formation, Pyrrhus defeated the Romans twice in 280 and 279 B.C.

E. After a fruitless campaign in Sicily, Pyrrhus returned to mainland Italy in 275 B.C. and fought the Romans to a standstill at Beneventum in 275.

F. Pyrrhus withdrew to his kingdom, leaving Rome mistress of all of the Italian peninsula south of the Po Valley.

IV. The expansion of Rome in Italy carried important ramifications for Roman politics, society, and culture.

A. The authority of the senate was greatly increased. Originally an advisory body made up of the wealthiest and most influential Romans, by the time of Pyrrhus' invasion, the senate had become the dominant political entity in the state. This was a consequence of the constant warfare, which placed a premium on experienced commanders.

B. There was great economic growth, as reflected in population increases, more building in Rome, increase in luxury goods, increase in the number of slaves, and so on.

C. There was cultural change, in the form of greater contacts with the Etruscans and, especially, the Greeks.

Essential Reading:

Livy, *Early History of Rome*, books 4–5.

T. J. Cornell, *The Beginnings of Rome*, chapters 12, 14.

Supplemental Reading:

A. Alföldi, *Early Rome and the Latins*.

E. T. Salmon, *Samnium and the Samnites*.

Questions to Consider:

1. Was Roman expansion in Italy a conscious campaign of conquest with long-term objectives set at the outset? If not, how can the Roman conquest of Italy be characterized?

2. Did the non-Roman peoples of Italy stand any chance against Roman aggression? If so, how? If not, why not?

Lecture Nine—Transcript
Roman Expansion In Italy

Welcome to the ninth lecture in The History of Ancient Rome. The last time we examined the Struggle of the Orders, an internal domestic dispute within the Roman Republic, a fledgling republic, although it lasted some 200 years. I mentioned at the end that throughout the period we were focused on the internal workings of the Roman State, externally, the Romans were extremely active militarily. It is to their expansion within Italy that I want to turn today.

Roman expansion in Italy can be broken down into three phases. First, there is a long period of gaining control over their immediate neighbors, the Latins, in the plane of Latium, south of Rome. That process came to a close in the middle of the fourth century B.C. Then the Romans trained their attention in earnest to central Italy, and specifically the difficult mountainous terrain of Samnium and the even more difficult, obdurate inhabitants, the Samnites, who were fearsome warriors and gave the Romans a run for their money in three wars, which saw Rome extend its power into central Italy. Then finally, Rome moved south and gained control over the Greek colonies in the south on the mainland, but not in Sicily. That is a different story. We will start this lecture with the Romans battling with their immediate neighbors and leave them in control of the entire Italian peninsula south of the Po Valley.

The stories of the Roman kings contain numerous legends and tales of the kings fighting their Latin neighbors. In fact, getting control of Latium proved to be Rome's most difficult task. It was an enterprise that went on for the best part of four centuries. At this time, in the earliest sources, we have accounts of kings mixing war and diplomacy, sometimes attacking, sometimes signing treaties with their immediate neighbors. We hear that the transition from monarchy to republic somewhat weakened the Roman position. Remember, the story of Lars Porsenna attacking Rome shortly after the expulsion of the Tarquins, and in one version of that tradition, taking the city, capturing it. But, they restored equilibrium; at least they restored their control over the Latins with the Battle of Lake Regillus of 499 B.C., which is presented to us as the third and final attempt of Tarquinius Superbus to gain entrance back into Rome. As far as external affairs go it allows us to see the Romans restoring their position of dominance, or at least their position of high influence over their immediate neighbors in Latium.

Shortly after the Battle of Lake Regillus came a landmark in their dealings with the Latins, which has come down to us as the *foedus Cassianum*, the Treaty of Cassius, named after the man who signed it. This treaty is presented to us in outline in some of our sources (some of our sources give us details). We hear from an offhand remark in Cicero, writing in the first century B.C., that a copy of this treaty was to be seen and read in the Forum in his day. This suggests, as we mentioned earlier, that probably accessible to our later authors was material far older which is now lost to us. It may, to some degree, offset our suspicions as to the reliability about these early events.

The outline of the treaty is pretty much as follows. The Treaty of Cassius was a mutual non-aggression pact. It was a military alliance. The Romans and Latins agreed that they would not attack each other, and that they would treat the same people as enemies and friends. They would unite together and defend each other if need be. Most importantly, they would share equally all the spoils of any war that they undertook together. The treaty also seems to have stipulated that in the case of any joint enterprises, Romans would command joint forces. The greatest uncertainty surrounds the issue of whether or not the Romans are to be seen as equal to the Latins in this treaty, whether they are members of what modern scholars call the Latin League, the agreement of individual Latin states to work together. Whether the Romans are a member of that league, just one vote among many, for instance, or whether the Romans stand outside the league, and the Treaty of Cassius is a bilateral agreement between the Romans and all of the Latins organized into their league, which would give the Romans much greater influence and control over events. The latter seems to be the case as far as we can tell, especially for the stipulation that joint forces are to be commanded by Romans.

In the years following the signing of the treaty—actually starting slightly beforehand—roughly from 500 B.C. to about 440 B.C., the Romans and the Latins found themselves occupied with fighting off incursions from the mountain dwellers to the east and south, tribal cultures called Aequi and Volsci, tough tribal fighters who would come down from the mountains during the campaigning season and raid the fertile plains even though these were on the outskirts of the city itself. The Romans are joining up with the Latins to face this threat together, and are in constant annual warfare with these tribal peoples. Since Romans commanded joint forces, this process of continual warfare helped give the Romans a sense of ascendancy over their Latin neighbors. At the same time they were fighting off the Volsci and Aequi to the south in defensive campaigns, the Romans were energetically embarked in campaigns to the north against their Etruscan neighbors, particularly the Etruscan town of Veii which was considerably more powerful than Rome at this early stage, the fifth century B.C., and allowed the conflict to go on for a protracted period of time. Having repulsed the Aequi and Volsci sufficiently so that the threat was neutralized the Romans more energetically turned their attention toward the north, using combined Latin and Roman armies to attack their northern neighbors. By 396 B.C., they had proven themselves very successful. In fact, they captured and destroyed Veii, but in an act of unbridled greed, the Romans took all the spoils of that war for themselves.

This act of arrogance was on the point of causing warfare between the Latins and the Romans when disaster struck from the north. We have seen that the area of the Po Valley in the north was considered by the Romans not to be part of Italy at all. They named it Gallia Cisalpina, Gaul, this side of the Alps. This is the area we consider to be in northern Italy today, the Northern Plains, was in that time occupied by Celtic tribesmen, Gauls. In 319 B.C., a large force of Gauls came out of Gallia Cisalpina and headed south. A Roman and Latin force hastily brought together to block this threat was crushed at the battle of the River Allia, and Rome lay open to the Gallic invaders. In outline, the Gauls took the city. In our stories, they destroyed the place, burned it to the ground, and the Romans came within a hairsbreadth of considering abandoning the site altogether and moving somewhere else.

In other words, this was in our sources, presented as a catastrophe. But, in a wonderful twist, it is presented as a heroic catastrophe. In the same way that many cultures will turn an abject failure into something noble, the same way in our worse hour we display many of our greatest traits. If we think of the Second World War, the disaster at Dunkirk preserves that tradition—the battle of Gettysburg for the Confederates in the South, the siege of Masada for the ancient Israelites and modern Israelis alike. The notion of the heroic failure is quite a powerful one, and the Gallic catastrophe is one of several Roman heroic failures. The stories surrounding the Gallic catastrophe are well worth telling. I wish I had the time to tell them to you. There are all kinds of wonderful vignettes and images from this event that have come down to us from the sources. I'll just pick two of my favorites. As the people are evacuating Rome, fleeing out the gates to get away, after news has come that the army at the Allia has been crushed, a simple plebeian, a man called Albinius takes his family in a cart. Seeing the Vestal Virgins carrying the sacred objects from the hearth of Rome with them he takes pity on them, takes his family out of the cart, puts the Vestals in with the sacred objects and allows them to be driven in style to refuge in the nearby town.

Even better, there are the eight imperious Roman nobles, who are too old to fight, who refused to enter into the last stand of the Capitoline Hill, the last stand of the fortress of the city of Rome. They refused to go in since they don't want to stretch the already restrained resources of the town, and maybe threaten the effectiveness of the defense. So, they sit in the vestibules of their houses in full stately regalia and await the onslaught of the Gauls. There is a superb moment described when one nobleman, Marcus Hyperius by name, is sitting in his house in full gear and a Gallic band comes into his house. You must imagine this. The Gauls fought naked, with mud in their hair. They would have looked more frightening than the punks do today, only armed with enormous swords and extremely aggressive attitudes. The Romans by stature were extremely small people. So, you have this large Gallic band of warriors. Hyperius stands up, looking down his nose at them. The Gaul comes over and tugs on his beard for which he gets slapped across the face for his insolence, which prompts the Gauls to slaughter Hyperius and his family where they stood—great images of the Roman sense of superiority. It must be said, however, that excavations at Rome have failed to verify widespread destruction at this time. If the city was burned to the ground, there is no sign of it in the archaeological record. Most scholars today believe that what happened was the Gauls came to Rome, looted the place, ransacked it, were perhaps bought off with a large bribe and then left. The Gauls weren't interested in occupying Rome; they just wanted some loot.

The Gallic raid humiliated Rome, but did not seem to have greatly deterred them from their chosen course of expansion over their neighbors. In the years following the Gallic raid, they built a seven-mile stretch of walls around the city. This is another sign, by the way, that the Romans were not as devastated by the Gallic catastrophe as they would have us believe. It is not the act of a defeated and crushed people to build a large stone fortification seven miles in circumference around their town. Clearly the Roman power hadn't been broken even if the Romans lost considerable face by the incident. Not going into detail, the Roman incursions into Etruria to the north and Latium to the south continued as relations with the Latins reached a peak in the Latin war of 341–338 B.C., which finally saw the Romans establish control over their Latin neighbors. By the date 238 B.C., the Romans had absorbed and conquered the Latins.

With the control over Latium secured, the Romans turned their attention to their southern/western flank where they found the Samnites. The Samnites were a formidable opponent. They were one of those Iron Age cultures that we talked about earlier in this course. They were a warrior society, tough fighters, as mountain men tend to be throughout history. They had initially signed a non-aggression pact with the Romans, but had then turned their attention to raiding the area of Campania, the plain south of Rome to the plain around Naples. Raiding into Campania resulted in the locals in that area appealing to Rome. This is an interesting fact. It seems that Rome has been recognized as a force to be reckoned with in the Italian geopolitical scene. So, when the Campanians felt pressed, they appealed to Roman for assistance, and in 343 B.C. the first Samnite war took place. It lasted only two years and was a rather indecisive affair and resulted in a renewal of the Romano/Samnite Treaty of some years prior.

However, with Roman control over Latium, and now with somewhat of a foothold over the Campanians in the south, the Romans began to extend their powers around the borders of traditional Samnite territory. They did so predominantly by founding cities and colonies at the boundaries of Samnite territory, squeezing the Samnites and putting them under pressure.

The Samnites weren't blind to this, and as a result, in 326 B.C., the Great, or Second, Samnite War broke out. This was a more serious conflict than the Romans had fought to date. It lasted over 20 years. It was a tumultuous struggle and showed the Romans sharply defeated on a number of fronts but continuously coming back and continuing the war in the face of whatever odds could be thrown at them. In 321 B.C., one of the worst humiliations in Roman history took place. A Roman army, under the consuls was trapped in a valley in Samnite territory. The Samnites lived in the central part of Italy, in the Apennines, very mountainous territory, very hard terrain to fight over. They knew it well and the Romans didn't. So, the Samnite general managed to trap a Roman army in the valley, and it was forced to surrender. The Romans were then stripped of their armor, which is a great humiliation for an ancient warrior if you remember that you have to provide your own equipment. You are essentially being mugged on a large scale. If that wasn't enough, they were forced to undergo a ritual of humiliation by being forced to march under a yoke used to connect oxen to a plow. This is apparently symbolic of the Romans being equivalent to pack animals. This is a tremendous humiliation. The Samnite army, fully armed, stood around and mocked them as this process went on, and it was long remembered in Roman history.

It only fueled Roman desire to continue the war, and by a combination of diplomacy and military operations, by 304 B.C., they had secured the surrender of the Samnites and nominally, the old treaty was renewed. In reality, Roman power now extended into Samnia. The Samnites had been now twice defeated by the Romans.

Not long afterwards, within six years, the third Samnite war had broken out. It seems that Roman wars come in groups of three. They are continuously having first, second and third wars with people. The third Samnite war lasted from 298 to 290 B.C., and in many ways it is something of a misnomer. With the end of the second Samnite War, Roman power now extended not only over Latium, it extended into all of central Italy and was now encroaching into Campania as well. Anyone with any sense would have realized what was happening. So, when the third Samnite war broke out, it quickly developed into a sort of pan-Italic resistance to the threat of Roman expansion. An enormous battle, the largest battle fought to date on the soil of Italy took place in 295 B.C. when a Roman army faced a coalition of Samnites, Umbrians, Etruscans, and even Gauls from the Po Valley who had united in an attempt to stop Roman expansion in Italy. We hear that the Romans fielded an army of some 36,000 men, but they faced an army of 100,000.

Remarkably, the Romans prevailed. This is the battle of Centinum, and in many ways marks the last stand to free Italy against Roman expansion. Following this, Roman control over all of central Italy from the area south of the Po Valley down to the Greek colonies in the south was secured. The war dragged on to 290 B.C., but at the end of that period, the Samnites were fully incorporated into the Roman state in a manner which we will examine in the next lecture on the Roman system of administration of their conquered territories. Roman control, however, over all of Italy was not yet secured. There were still the Greek colonies in the south of Italy.

One of these colonies was that of Tarentum right in the heel, the instep of Italy if you think of it as a boot or shoe. This place had been worried by Roman expansion for some time, and finally, in 280 B.C. found itself facing the extension of Roman power south from Campania. In particular, the Romans made an agreement with a neighboring and rival state of Tarentum called Thurii. They made an agreement with that state and the Tarentines understood to be a direct threat to themselves. With Thurii aligned with the Romans, Thurii faced a serious threat to their security because Thurii was one of their rivals.

Feeling that they were unable to face the Romans and their control over Italy alone, the Tarentines appealed to one of the more colorful characters in ancient history, a man with the glorious name of Pyrrhus of Epirus. That is King Pyrrhus of the kingdom of Epirus which was across the Adriatic Sea along the shores of what would now be considered parts of former Yugoslavia, Albania, and Macedonia. Pyrrhus was a young, energetic and ambitious king, a Greek king of the Hellenistic model who when he got the invitation to come over to Italy was only too happy to accept the chance for some military adventure across the sea. In 281 B.C., he arrived with an army of 25,000 highly trained troops who fought in the formidable formation, the Macedonian Phalanx, which was really an extremely formidable military formation. He also brought with him something the Romans had never seen before: elephants—he brought 20 elephants with him.

Pyrrhus' well-equipped, highly-trained, Greek-style army was certainly something that the Romans had never fought before. They were used to fighting tribal peoples in Italy. This was a quasi-professional force. The Greek phalanx, or the Macedonian version of the Greek phalanx was an incredibly powerful ancient tactic. It involved ranks of men, sometimes going back 18 deep, with vast pikes, extending out 20 or 30 feet in length. It presented something like a hedgehog of spears to the enemy, which would advance en masse across the field and literally shove an opponent off the field, just walk right over them. You have eighteen ranks of troops marching shoulder to shoulder with enormous pikes looking like an enormous porcupine coming at you. If there are elephants involved in the mix, that is all the worse. The elephants come first, scatter your lines, and then there is the Greek phalanx marching down on top of you. So, they were a very formidable force. In two quick battles in 280 and 279 B.C., Pyrrhus succeeded in defeating the Romans. The story goes that because of the enormous casualties incurred in fighting these battles, Pyrrhus was being congratulated by one of his lieutenants, who said "Sire, congratulations on a fine victory over the Romans," and his response was "One more victory like that, and we are done for." This has given rise to the phrase a "Pyrrhic Victory," a victory that is not worth winning because it costs so much.

The Tarentines in rather fickle fashion, once they had seen the Romans defeated, figured that Pyrrhus had outlived his usefulness and turned their backs on the man they had invited over to help them. Pyrrhus got restless and took off into Sicily. Following his defeat of the Romans in 279, he went down into Sicily for some military adventure, but proved himself to be rather ineffective there. He did not really succeed in doing anything in particular, and came back into Italy again at the invitation of the Greeks in the south who were feeling the pressure of the Romans in 275 B.C. Another major battle was fought against the Romans, this time with no decisive outcome. This battle was fought at Beneventum in south central Italy. It convinced Pyrrhus that his campaigns against the Romans in Italy were a fruitless endeavor, so he departed for his kingdom. He was killed in an extremely ludicrous fashion later in his life. Whilst attacking neighboring towns near the Balkan region and entering one of them which he had taken. A woman threw a tile down from a roof and hit him on the head and killed him.

With the withdrawal of Pyrrhus from Italy and subsequent diplomatic maneuvers, the Romans had by 270 B.C. secured control over the entire Italian peninsula south of the Po Valley. If it took the Romans 400 years to control the Plain of Latium, they had gained control over the rest of Italy in under 70. It was a meteoric rise to power and was to be overshadowed by the even more extraordinary feats they were to perform on the international stage in the decades to follow.

The expansion of Rome in Italy carried several important ramifications for Roman society and politics that we should look at to close out the lecture. In the first place, the authority of the Senate was greatly enhanced by the continuous warfare. The Senate appears originally to have been an ad hoc ad advisory committee to the king which then became a standing advisory body to the magistrates comprised of the most influential Romans that there were. As a result the Senate contained within its ranks all of the experienced generals of the Roman state, not to mention the wealthiest and best educated people of the Roman state. With the continuous warfare of these years, the prestige of the senate and its grip over Roman politics was greatly enhanced. Naturally enough, if there is continuous warfare, one will pay close attention to what one's generals and ex-generals have to say. Although the senate was technically an advisory body, its political control over the Roman state was greatly enhanced by the wars of expansion in Italy and was to be even further enhanced by the international war that Rome was about to embark upon. It is important to restate that the control or the high position of the Roman senate in the Roman State was a product of circumstances, not of constitutionality or the passage of laws. It was a product of circumstances.

The Senate rose in prestige. Also, there was tremendous economic growth, naturally enough, as an offshoot of Roman expansion in Italy. We see the population of the city rising in this time. There is evidence of more building going on in Rome, larger and bigger public buildings being erected from archaeological excavations. We find a greater concentration of luxury goods turning up. There seems to have been a concomitant rise in the number of slaves. It is not exactly un-coincidental that debt-bondage was abolished in 326 B.C. just around the time the Romans were being successful against the Samnites in expanding their power in central Italy and had access to more slaves. Who needs debt bondage when you have slave labor? As a result, it does seem that slaves increased in number and frequency in the Roman state at this time.

The final ramification of the Roman expansion in Italy must be the great cultural change that the Romans underwent at this time. They had been familiar with Greek culture through the Etruscans. Now, with having direct dealings with the Greek cities of southern Italy, in fact being in the position of controlling those cities, the level of Hellenization of the Romans began to increase, especially in the years following the wars against Pyrrhus from 270 B.C. onwards. That process of Hellenization was to pick up even greater pace when the Romans came to encounter the Greeks directly in their homeland in the eastern Mediterranean as they expanded their empire eastward. The expansion of Rome on the international scene is something that will occupy the next few lectures.

Lecture Ten
The Roman Confederation in Italy

Scope:

In this lecture we take a pause in our narrative to examine how the Romans administered their conquests in Italy. The system of administration, generally called the Roman Confederation of Italy, was complex and involved ranking subject communities in a hierarchy of status with regard to their relationship with Rome. The system formed the basis of Roman dealings with other subject peoples who had not yet come under their yoke, and it goes a long way toward explaining the longevity of the Roman Empire.

Outline

I. The Romans developed early in their history a system of privilege-sharing with allied or related communities that differed from the usually harsh treatment ancient victors showed to their vanquished foes.

   A. Although the origins of the system are obscure, it seems that the Romans could, under certain conditions, extend the privileges of citizenship to other communities.
   1. In later years it was not unusual for the Romans to extend the rights of citizenship to whole communities.
   2. This practice appears to have been present very early, as illustrated by the example of Gabii.
   3. By the third century B.C., a secondary citizenship status had emerged, the state without the vote (a citizenship lacking rights of political participation, called *civitas sine suffragio*).

   B. The Romans also embarked on a policy of colonization early in their history. Foundation of colonies was one important diplomatic wing of Roman expansion in Italy.
   1. Roman colonies were founded in newly conquered territories and at strategically important locations.
   2. Colonies were initially comprised of Romans and Latins, the former being the largest group.
   3. Colonists enjoyed what came to be called "Latin Rights" (*ius Latii*), which was a sort of restricted Roman citizenship.

4. The Roman foundation of colonies was carried on in peacetime, but it could be provocative, as when it contributed to the outbreak of the Second Samnite War.

C. As Roman power expanded, the Romans developed other degrees of community status (e.g., the "double colonies").

1. Beginning with Tusculum in 381 B.C., the Romans developed a community status below the colony, called the *municipium.*

2. The rights and status of a *municipium* in the early period are unclear, but in later periods the *municipium* comprised local citizens whose ruling classes alone were admitted to Roman citizenship.

3. Below the *municipium*, and especially in south Italy, the Romans established "treaty states" (*civitates foederatae*).

4. Treaty states enjoyed only those privileges stipulated in their treaty with Rome.

II. The developed Confederation of Italy allowed the Romans to "divide and conquer" the peoples of Italy, and it offered great benefits to the Romans.

A. The final form of the Confederation, as it had evolved over centuries, ranked subject communities in a variety of bilateral status-relationships with Rome.

1. The final form of the Confederation was as follows: at the top were colonies of Roman citizens (*optima iure*); next came Latin colonies (*ius Latii*); *municipia* stood below the Latin colonies; treaty states (*civitates foederatae*) brought up the rear.

2. Within this scheme, the Romans could promote or demote communities depending on circumstances.

3. Eventually, these statuses could be conferred by the Roman Senate on any community (e.g., colonial or Latin status could be granted to already existing communities).

B. These bilateral arrangements effectively divided the Italians among themselves.

    1. In each case, the agreements were bilateral between Rome and the subject communities, encouraging the locals to look to Rome for their welfare.

    2. Adjacent communities could enjoy widely divergent statuses with Rome, mitigating their capability to act in concert against Rome.

C. The system also provided Rome with a large pool of military manpower.

    1. Whatever the status of the subject community, provision of troops for the army was a universal requirement.

    2. Rome could therefore impose the basic duty of citizenship, military service, without offering the privileges of citizenship in every case.

    3. Thus, approximately half of the Roman army came from the subject states of the Roman Confederation of Italy.

III. This early system of administration of conquered territories had several important long-term consequences.

A. It was to play a vital role in facilitating Roman overseas expansion, by virtue of the huge manpower Rome could bring to bear on any given situation.

B. In times of crisis, it offered Rome security, as when Pyrrhus failed to detach Rome's allies from the Confederation or during the Second Punic War (Lecture 13).

C. When an altered version of the Confederation was extended beyond Italy, it was to form the basis for the stability and longevity of the later Roman Empire. (* See note at end of Lecture 10 outline)

Essential Reading:

T. J. Cornell, *The Beginnings of Rome*, chapter 12.

Supplemental Reading:

A. N. Sherwin-White, *The Roman Citizenship*, esp. chapters 1–2.

Questions to Consider:

1. What criteria did Rome apply in determining the status of subject communities?

2. To what degree did Roman political domination of Italy entail a cultural domination of the peninsula?

---

* *Erratum*: On the tape, the professor states that the Byzantine Empire fell in A.D. 1454. The correct date is A.D. 1453.

Lecture Ten—Transcript
The Roman Confederation in Italy

Hello and welcome to the tenth lecture in The History of Ancient Rome. In the last lecture we examined the rise of Rome to political and military dominance in the Italian peninsula. We saw how the Romans took the best part of four centuries to be in control of their immediate neighbors in Latium, then spent only 70 years conquering the rest of the peninsula. It was quite a meteoric and impressive achievement. What I want to do today is pause before we look at the broader picture of Mediterranean politics and then look at the beginnings of Rome's rise to world power (by ancient standards). What I wish to do is pause before we look at that and examine the system of administration that the Romans evolved for their control of the conquered territories in Italy. This was essential to their later success and was also a contributing factor to the overall longevity of their empire as a whole.

The standard treatment of conquered territories or communities in the ancient Mediterranean world was harsh. The norm would have been for the defeated city to be destroyed and looted, the adult male population to be executed, and the women and children to be sold into slavery. This was the common practice among Greek warring city-states. There were exceptions, but quite frequently, resistance was crushed down in the most brutal and severe fashion. The Romans were not averse to doing this sort of thing if the resistance of their opponents had been especially obdurate or difficult.

What makes them remarkable is that they evolved apparently quite early in their career in imperialism a method of privilege sharing with their territories. This, over the course of their rise to power in Italy, became a unique system of confederation that united the Italian communities that had been defeated by Rome into a broader system of alliances with varying degrees of status in their relationship with Rome between the communities that had been conquered and the Romans themselves. This is generally termed the Roman Confederation of Italy, and it stands at the root of Roman imperial success in the Mediterranean. First, we will outline the nature of that system as best we can. You won't be surprised to hear that the early origins of that system and the early shape of it are unclear to us given the nature of our sources for this early period. Having done that, we will examine its ramifications and consequences for Rome and for Italy.

It seems that the Romans adopted the system of privilege sharing fairly early. We hear that Tarquinius Superbus, the last king of Rome, signed a treaty with the neighboring town of Gabii, a Latin community, which included a clause giving Gabii equal citizen rights with the Romans. The technical term is *isopolity*, equal rights of citizenship with the Romans. By the third century B.C., the Romans had evolved a secondary style of citizenship. I won't call it second-class citizenship, but a level below full citizenship which they called citizenship without the vote, *civitas sine suffragio*, citizenship without the right of taking part in the political system. The origins of this system remain somewhat unclear, but it does seem to have been in place by roughly 300 B.C. Another parallel line of development that the Romans embarked upon apparently very early in their history was a system of colonization. We mentioned earlier the Greek colonies in the south of Italy and pointed out how the Greek colonies whether in Italy or the eastern Mediterranean were independent city-states. They weren't part of an imperial polity by the Greeks. They weren't instruments of control.

This is not the case with the Roman colonies. Roman colonies are instruments of empire. The colonies set out by the Romans within Italy and eventually outside Italy were means of control for the Romans to establish garrisons in conquered territories, also to introduce the Roman style of life, Roman urbanized culture, to non-urbanized parts of the world especially when they found themselves in control of areas like France and Spain that were controlled at this time by Iron Age tribal cultures. In the earliest years, it seems the colonies were a means of establishing a firm Roman foothold in conquered territories. They were often located at strategic locations. It seems that prior to 338 B.C., the colonies were originally comprised of a group of families of Roman citizens with a group of families of Latin allies sent out together. Together, the whole community was given another form of quasi-citizenship called "The Latin Right," *jus latii,* which is a more restricted form of citizenship than the *civitas sine suffragio*, than the citizenship without the vote. I will deal with that in a second.

Following the final subjugation of the Latins in 338 B.C., the Romans also began to establish colonies of pure Roman citizens, sending out colonies just made up of full Roman citizens. These colonies were founded outside the original Latin territory and seem to have been located at strategic locations. Many are to be found along the coast, and they are often called Maritime Colonies for that reason. They seem to have been places where the Romans were eager to secure their coastal territory, to make sure they would be safe from any sea-born attacks from any enemies. Again, these are strategic instruments of empire, whether they are Latin colonies or full citizen colonies.

The system of colonization which had been ongoing from earliest times, modified slightly after 338 B.C., continued down to around the early part of the second century when it stopped. It was not to be revived again until the first century B.C., as we will see in the context of the Roman revolution. We will see it then revived in slightly modified form so that by the first century B.C., we have no less than three different styles of colonies. We have colonies of full Roman citizens. We have colonies with the Latin rights, and finally we have a new form of colony that became popular in the first century B.C. called the double colony. This is the insertion of a group of Roman citizen colonists into an existing community. You have a double community. You have the people who were citizens of their town before the Romans came living side-by-side with a group of Roman colonists in their midst. These are often called double colonies.

I mention all this to show you that this is a complex and evolutionary process, a process that reflects something deeper about the Romans themselves. I might as well mention it now because we will be seeing it again in the future. That is the remarkably adaptive and pragmatic nature of the Romans when it comes to matters administrative. They were always willing to change their way of doing things to suit new circumstances. This system of colonization did not just pop out of someone's head. It evolved over several centuries. Latin rights evolved for specific reasons. Colonies of Roman citizens evolved for specific reasons and under certain circumstances, and double colonies likewise.

So, they are always adapting and changing their way of doing things, modifying them in order to optimize the benefits to themselves and their control over conquered territories. This adaptive nature of the Romans is one of their cardinal characteristics and one of the reasons for their success as imperialists. I should mention that the establishment of colonies was quite a big business. Officials would be assigned to go out and find a spot. Colonies are usually founded on virgin soil. The exception is the double colonies where the colonists are inserted into an existing colony.

By and large, Latin and full-Roman citizen colonies are established in a virgin spot. A board of officers is established to go out and chart the spot to demarcate the places where the plots of land will be, where the main center of town will be and so forth. Then the colonists are grouped together. They are assigned plots of land in the new territory. They all go out together. Very important religious rituals take place to notify the gods that a new community of Roman citizens and devotees is being established that will require their protection. The boundaries of the colony are set, usually all surrounded by religious ritual, and then the colony starts to construct itself and build its urban center. Then the families move in and start farming. It is quite a big business surrounded by a lot of hullabaloo, and one must imagine it must have been a time of considerable excitement as well as a very useful way for the Romans to siphon off excess population from their city themselves. It is very handy to have the ability to establish new communities and siphon off the landless people accumulating in Rome. Remember we are in an age long before social welfare or anything even like it. If you have a large population that is not doing a lot in your community, that is a burden to the community. So, it is very handy to be able to siphon these people off and establish them in new towns and cities around Italy.

We mentioned the Latin rights. This is also a subject or process that is shrouded in uncertainty at its roots. It becomes clearer to us later, when it is a more complex system because it has gone through the process of adaptation and evolution I have mentioned. It seems that in its earliest stages, the Latin rights, *jus latii*, comprised the ability of people who were living in Latium who were not granted full citizenship by the Romans to enjoy certain privileges of citizenship without enjoying all the rights of citizenship. One of the most interesting things about Latin rights was the potential for naturalization. One could move to Rome, register in Rome as a Latin citizen and then be upgraded to be a full citizen.

Another feature of the Latin rights that seems to be very early was the right of inter-marriage with full citizens. One had the right to marry a woman of full citizen stock, and any children that were produced would be full citizens. The Romans then modified and changed the system of Latinity. The colonial Latin right was the same in every respect as the earlier Latin right only that it lacked the right of inter-marriage. That was something they decided that, for whatever reason, had to be withdrawn from the colonial Latin status. It is a process of adaptation and evolution. It is quite difficult for us to make out how the system evolved simply because our sources are so poor for the earliest period. Clearly, as with the colonies, here we have the Romans thinking hard about how they are governing their conquered territories and above all, privilege sharing—some of the privileges of being a Roman citizen. This is really what was quite unique by ancient standards in the Roman treatment of conquered territories. They did not just crush them underfoot, there was an element of attempting to partially integrate the conquered peoples into the state of Rome.

If we move along, we can see that the foundation of Roman colonies continued to pace with Roman expansion and could lead to conflict. We saw yesterday that the second Samnite war broke out because the Romans were founding colonies right on the borders of Samnium. The Samnites recognized this as a direct threat to themselves. As a result, the Second Samnite War evolved. So, it seems that the imperialist motive behind the founding of colonies was recognized even by the Italians themselves as it was happening.

If we have communities with Latin rights, colonies, the Romans began to evolve another grade of community status below the Latin colony called the *municipium*, from which our word "municipality" comes from. The *municipium* first seems to have appeared in 381 B.C. with the town of Tusculum being given certain privileges and rights that weren't quite Latin rights but weren't quite citizen rights either. They weren't quite colonial rights.

In other words, it was something new, a new status for a community. It is very hard for us to identify the direct process of evolution that stands behind the development of the *municipium*, but in better documented times, in short, the *municipium* seems to be a sort of self-sustaining, existing community. It is not a new foundation, it is a self-sustaining, autonomous existing community in which the citizens of the town hold local citizenship. So, if we were to use a modern analogy, they would be citizens of Philadelphia, of Washington. They could vote for their local authorities within that township. Sometimes they were also given that citizenship without the vote of the broader Roman world. Sometimes they were given that. Often the magistrates, the ruling classes of the *municipium*, were given full Roman citizenship. That is very clever. If you think about the subtlety of that system, it basically co-ops the local ruling elite fully into the Roman citizenship body and ensures that the local elite who are already in control of the people will be loyal to you and your newly rising empire. That is an extremely clever mechanism for gaining control over the local towns of Italy.

At some stage in the third or maybe in the fourth century the Romans developed yet another level of community status below that of the *municipium* which they called *civitates foederatae*, treaty states. These were states which had a treaty with Rome that dictated specific individual privileges and duties that community owed to Rome and that Rome owed to that community. These treaty states were originally called "the allies" by the Romans, but that phrase *socii*, came to be applied to all of the Italian subject communities under Roman control by the second century B.C. The developed Italian confederation is a complex quilt, a complex, patchwork of community status. To review it again, in its developed form, (the second and first centuries B.C.) all the communities of Italy would have existed in a specific relationship with Rome. At the top are colonies of full Roman citizens organized into an independent community. Next came the Latin colonies, colonies with people who had Latin rights. Below the Latin colonies came the *municipia*, the local communities in which only the magistrates held full Roman citizenship and the citizen body may have had a lower class form of Roman citizenship, but were essentially members of their self-governing local communities. Below those came the treaty states whose rights and privileges were determined bilaterally in their arrangements with Rome.

What is so clever about the system is that there is always a potential for improvement. You have essentially a ladder of community status. If you start out as a treaty state, and you are a good little boy and do as the Romans insist, there is a possibility for you to be promoted by a vote of the Roman senate up the ladder. There is always a chance to better yourself, and the way to better yourself is to do what the Romans want you to do, an excellent system for controlling and marshalling the resources of Italy.

Eventually, these statuses, colonial, Latin and the status of a *municipium* could be conferred on any community by a vote of the Roman senate. It did not have to be a new foundation. Any community at all could be declared a colony of Roman citizens if the Romans decided it was so. This helped allow the subject peoples to recognize that they had a chance of betterment, of going up the ladder. It is important to stress that in every case, each of these arrangements are bi-lateral between Rome and the specific communities. This effectively encourages the locals to look toward Rome for their betterment. It directs the loyalties of the subject communities toward Rome.

As a result, adjacent communities could have widely divergent statuses in their relationships with Rome. It would be possible to have a full colony of Roman citizens, a *municipium*, and a treaty state all within a single locality, but all enjoying widely divergent status relationships with Rome. This would discourage those communities from working in concert against Rome. Why should a colony of Roman citizens throw in their hat with a treaty state when they are already doing quite well out of the Roman confederation of Italy.

A cardinal benefit to the Romans of this entire system and one that was at the root of their success in empire was that whatever the relationship or status of the subject community, the fundamental requirement the Romans demanded of you was the supply of men for their army. The fundamental requirement of being subject to the Romans was to supply men for their army. They may or may not tax you.

Full Roman citizen colonies were not taxed. Many *municipia* could enjoy tax immunity. Treaty states often were subject to tax in tribute. Whatever your status, you had to supply a levy of troops when the time came. How precisely this was done, we can't say. It seems that the Romans would simply declare at the start of every new campaigning season, around February or March of every year, they would send out a message to their allies to produce X number of troops, of course fully equipped, because you would bring your own equipment. They should show up at this spot on this day, and then we will go off beating up on our neighbors. What we can say is that during the Roman Republic, Roman armies typically had half of their manpower provided by the Italian allies. You can see how important this system is to the Romans. If you are embarking on an imperial enterprise, it is very useful to be able to effectively double your manpower by marshalling the resources of your subject communities.

Why did the Italians comply? They would be induced to fight not only on the threat of punishment if they refused. They could also be induced to loyalty by the promise of loot and spoils if the Romans were victorious, which they tended to be. Sometimes there could be other benefits. If a community's soldiers fought bravely and well, and this was noticed by the Roman general or consul in control of the army, then the whole community could be rewarded by an upgrade in the community statuses that applied in Italy. So, there were many positive inducements for the Italians to fight with the Romans. We can say for sure that Roman armies of the republic were typically 50 percent Italian allies. However it was that the specific levy for a specific community was determined, that aside, we do know that they were always able to draw up enough troops to provide at least half of the manpower for their armies. This federated system really allowed the Romans to impose one of the basic dues of citizenship— that is to say military service on people without giving everyone all the privileges of full citizenship as well. Again, it is a very clever system that allows the Romans to marshal the resources of Italy without being completely profligate with their citizenship.

The system of administration of Italy and the conquered territories there had several important long-term consequences for the Romans. It was an absolutely vital part of their ability to expand overseas. This was by virtue of the enormous pool of manpower that the Romans could draw on. We have already seen a hint of this when we saw Pyrrhus' invasion of Italy in 281 B.C. Pyrrhus came over with a large well-trained Macedonian army and elephants just for good measure, and defeated the Romans in two major battles albeit with severe losses to themselves. In the first two encounters that the Romans had with Pyrrhus, they were defeated. This would have been in normal circumstances (if Pyrrhus had been dealing with a sane community) the end of the war. With two major defeats, the next natural, logical pattern of events would have been that Pyrrhus would have waited in his tent. Romans would have shown up; they would have negotiated a peace, perhaps ceding some territory to Pyrrhus in Italy, and that would have been the end of the war.

Instead, Pyrrhus went into this tent and all that came were more Roman armies. The Romans simply refused to negotiate and they could draw up yet another army to send against Pyrrhus. This dogged feature of Roman resistance which was also characteristic of the war against Hannibal as we will see in a future lecture, is in no small measure a product of their knowledge that they have a vast pool of manpower to draw upon. If one army gets crushed, there is plenty more where that came from. It allowed them in their overseas conquests to conduct campaigns often simultaneously in different parts of the Mediterranean world. No other ancient state at this time could have marshaled the manpower resources to carry out such widespread operations or to have refused to negotiate after two major defeats at the hands of an invading power. So, the manpower element benefit of the Roman Confederation is a cardinal benefit of the Roman system of administration of Italy.

Another major benefit is that in times of crisis, the confederation offered Rome great security. We will see this drawn out very clearly with the war against Hannibal when a foreign general is stomping around Italy. We will see that the allies sticking by the Romans is a key reason for their success. In fact, it is in the time of crisis that the success of the Romans in marshalling the loyalties of the Italians is really drawn out. This is when the value of their careful construction of this federated system within Italy is really brought to the fore. When they are threatened with ultimate destruction and their allies stand by them. Not one ally offered to go over to Pyrrhus when he invaded. There were some defections to Hannibal as we will see, but the core of the Roman Confederation in central Italy stood firm even in the face of massive defeats inflicted on the Romans by Hannibal and the Carthaginians on Italian soil. It is a remarkable story and remarkable testament to the success of the Roman Confederation of Italy.

Another long-term consequence of this is what it reveals fundamentally about Roman attitude toward their treatment of conquered people which was to be at the root of the success of their empire and especially of its longevity. Unique among large empires, the Romans, when they finally found themselves in control of a very large empire, extended this system of privilege sharing outside the empire. As a result, they managed to create a massive political unit in which people whether they lived in Syria or Scotland considered themselves to be Romans and felt that they were a part of a single political and cultural entity, even if there was plenty of diversity within the details of the fully developed, fully extended Roman Empire. The whole notion that people were Romans was a very powerful one and has its roots in this system of confederation and privilege sharing in Italy. Even as the Turks were bashing down the walls of Constantinople in 1454 [sic 1453], the Byzantines inside Constantinople were calling themselves Romaoi (Romans) still. This achievement of the Romans in marshalling the loyalties of the subject peoples of an enormous international empire has its roots in their treatment of the Italian communities.

Italy in 270 B.C. on the eve of Roman expansion across the Mediterranean looks like a quilt of varying statuses, communities in varying statuses with Rome, all of them (this is the point that really has to be driven home) with the obligation and requirement of supplying the Roman armies with men, which as we will see shortly were to be put to energetic use in the years to come.

Lecture Eleven
The International Scene on the
Eve of Roman Expansion

Scope:

In this lecture we focus on the international geopolitical situation as it stood in 264 B.C., on the eve of Rome's rise to an overseas empire. After a preliminary overview of the sources, we see that the Mediterranean world was divided into power bases, east and west. Carthage was the dominant power in the west, while in the east a variety of Hellenistic kingdoms competed with each other in the military and diplomatic spheres. Few of these powers could have imagined that land-based Rome was about to emerge from Italy and defeat them all.

Outline

I. Our sources for Roman history from ca. 270 B.C. onward improve greatly.

   A. There are improved literary sources, notably Polybius, Livy, Dionysius of Halicarnassus, and Cassius Dio. These writers often had available contemporary or near-contemporary sources now lost to us.

   B. There are more frequent inscriptions of all sorts. (Note: for details on these authors, please refer to the Biographical Notes.)

   C. Archaeological evidence becomes more abundant.

II. The geopolitical situation in the Mediterranean in c. 270 B.C. was complex.

   A. In the western Mediterranean lay Carthage and the Greek colonies on Syracuse.

   1. Carthage was a powerful mercantile naval state with links throughout the western Mediterranean.

   2. The Greek colonies on Sicily, especially Syracuse, were ancient and formidable.

   3. Much of the rest of the west, particularly the hinterland and northern reaches of Western Europe, were under tribal societies of Celts and Germans.

B. The eastern Mediterranean was the ancient home of civilization.

    1. The eastern Mediterranean had a history of civilization stretching back 3000 years.

    2. Egypt, Syria, Asia Minor (Turkey), and Greece all had long heritages of organized and urbanized statehood.

    3. The situation in this region in c. 270 B.C. was itself complex.

C. Alexander the Great's conquests had created the Hellenistic kingdoms in this region.

    1. Alexander's conquest of Persia was followed by turmoil in the eastern lands.

    2. Alexander's generals vied with one another, initially for control of the empire, but later for what part of it they could safely control.

    3. The result was a balance of power among three mutually antagonistic Hellenic kingdoms ruled by descendants of Alexander's generals: in Egypt ruled the Ptolemaic Dynasty; in Syria ruled the Seleucids; in the Macedonian homeland ruled the Antigonids.

    4. In the buffer zones between these major states, smaller kingdoms and federations arose, *viz.*, the Aetolian and Achaean Leagues held sway in mainland Greece; the Attalid kingdom of Pergamum ruled in northwest Asia Minor; the third entity was the island state of Rhodes.

D. These Hellenistic states were sophisticated and were constantly in competition with one another. Smaller states survived by allying themselves with more powerful ones, or by playing one off the other.

III. In this complex international scene, the rise of Rome in Italy was not a major event.

    A. For the most part these important and historical states paid little attention to Rome's rise to dominance in Italy.

    B. There were two exceptions.

        1. Carthage is reported to have made three treaties with Rome in 509, 348, and 306 B.C.

        2. These treaties, particularly the earliest, are disputed, but they appear to have been designed to protect Carthaginian interests in Italy.

3. In 273 B.C., the Ptolemaic dynasty in Egypt declared "friendship" with Rome, clearly a response to Pyrrhus's failure in Italy. This ensured the survival of Ptolemaic Egypt until 31 B.C.

C. There was little indication in ca. 270 B.C. that Rome was on the brink of conquering the entire Mediterranean basin, which it would do in little more than 100 years.

    1. The superpowers were Egypt and Syria in the east and Carthage in the west.

    2. Rome had a naval capacity, but it was not a major naval power.

    3. Rome had a coastal defense navy and had even fought some naval battles, but did not compare with the other big powers, including Rhodes and especially Carthage.

    4. Carthage became the first adversary of expanding Rome.

Essential Reading:

Cary and Scullard, *A History of Rome*, 113–16, 150–51.

Supplemental Reading:

E. S. Gruen, *The Hellenistic World and the Coming of Rome*.

Questions to Consider:

1. What factors can you identify in the shaping of the international scene in the Mediterranean prior to c. 270 B.C.?

2. How did Rome measure up as a major power on the eve of her expansion overseas? What advantages did it have for the coming struggles?

Lecture Eleven—Transcript
The International Scene on the
Eve of Roman Expansion

Hello and welcome to the eleventh lecture in The History of Rome. The last time we examined the growth of Roman power in Italy and specifically the system of administration that the Romans developed in Italy, often termed The Roman Confederation of Italy. We saw how it stood at the basis of Roman expansion for the rest of the Mediterranean world. I want to now turn our attention to the basis of that expansion, but before doing so, a couple of familiarity points. We are now approaching the core of the course. I mentioned at the start of the course that we would be focusing on the period roughly from 300 B.C. to A.D. 300. We are now entering that period. It is at this stage that our sources become so much better than they were before. I wish to look at those sources briefly before moving into setting the stage for the expansion of Rome across the Mediterranean world.

Our written sources improve enormously in this period because we have from the period around the 160s to the 150s B.C. an excellent source in the form of Polybius. He is our first extant, written source for the Roman world, for Roman history. There were earlier Roman historians, but they have all disappeared. For instance, the very first one we know about was a gentleman known as Quintus Fabius Pictor in the third century B.C. We know about him. He is referred to in later sources, but we have none of his work. So, it is nice to know that he was there, but it would be even nicer if we could read him. It is not until Polybius, in the middle of the second century, that we get a continuous account of Roman history.

Polybius was Greek. He had come to Rome primarily as a hostage, taken by the Romans as a hostage against his people, in 168 B.C. He was not held in a basement, chained to a wall or anything like that. Rather, he was treated with a great deal of respect and formed a friendship with one of the leading Roman families of the day, the Cornelii Scipiones, a leading patrician and consular family, and as a result was in a perfect position to observe the operations of the Romans at the very time that they were expanding their empire. In fact, it was to explain this rapid expanse of Rome across the Mediterranean that he wrote his histories in 40 books the purpose of which was to explain and document the rise of Rome in so short a time as 50 or so years from the end of the third century on into the second century. Only five books of those 40 survive intact. Others are known through excerpts and fragments quoted in other authors. So, we have a pretty good picture of Polybius' work overall. Overall, we are dealing with an educated, intelligent Greek mind observing Rome from the outside as well as from the inside. He is observing Rome from the outside insofar as he is not a Roman, but he is there at the heart of things, so he makes an invaluable source for our study of the rise of the Roman Empire.

We also have Livy whose work continues in this period—much of it based on Polybius. We have Dionysius of Halicarnassus who I have mentioned to you a few times already, who was writing about the same time as Livy in 30 B.C., or onwards in the decades following 30 B.C. He wrote 20 books called *Roman Antiquities*, which covered Roman history to the outbreak of the first Punic War. Eleven of those books survive, and he is also quite a useful source if slightly rhetorical and given to praising the Romans at every opportunity. Our last major source for this period is Cassius Dio. He is a man who lived far later, born in A.D. 164, died around A.D. 230. He was a Greek, but a senator who wrote an 80-book history of Rome from earliest times up to his own day which survive—some in full and the rest in summary form. He is more useful for the imperial period than for the republic, but he can supplement our written sources when needed.

In addition to the literary sources, at this time inscriptions become more abundant. These are inscriptions from the Greek world about the Romans, and from the Latin world itself. At this stage, the Romans have conquered Italy and their language, Latin, is becoming the dominant language of the peninsula, starting to suppress the pre-Roman languages that were around prior to the appearance of the Roman state in Italy. We basically get more abundant archaeological evidence. So, in other words, all our forms of evidence, epigraphical and archaeological, improve in the third century B.C. and continue to get better for the rest of the period covered in this course. So much for the sources.

Let us look now at the geopolitical situation in the Mediterranean, west first then the eastern side to examine what it was the world was like that the Romans were to conquer. The situation across the Mediterranean was highly complex. I think it can be easily and justifiably divided between west and east. In the western half of the Mediterranean, we have already seen the presence of the Greek colonies, in Italy and in Sicily. There were also a handful of Greek colonies further west, a notable one being the colony of Masalia in southern France, the modern day city of Marseilles and also one in northern Spain. The dominant rival colonists of the western Mediterranean to the Greeks had been the Phoenicians. The Phoenicians stem from the area of modern day Lebanon, and they had moved westward in the period around 1100 B.C. onwards. They founded a series of cities in the western Mediterranean. They were very enterprising seafarers, the Phoenicians. They circumnavigated the continent of Africa and signs of them have been found as far north as Cornwall in England. So, they went out into the Atlantic Ocean and sailed there. They are extremely enterprising merchant-based people. Around 800 B.C., they founded a city in modern day Tunisia in northern Africa, which is known as Carthage. This Phoenician colony was to become a dominant force in the western Mediterranean. We look at Carthage in more detail in the next lecture when we examine the outbreak of war between Rome and Carthage, but suffice it to say that by the time the Romans had conquered all of Italy, Carthage was probably the major power in the western Mediterranean area.

The Greek colonies in Sicily knew the power of Carthage, because they had spent many generations fighting them. The Carthaginians, and the Greeks, especially Syracuse in Sicily, had fought many and long wars over control of that island. We should not forget that the Greeks were also around the Greek colonies of Italy still independent of Roman power. The Romans had conquered the mainland of the Italian peninsula so they had taken over places like Naples and Tarentum. The major power of Syracuse, probably the most powerful of the Greek city-states anywhere was still an independent state at this early stage of the third century B.C. As for the west of the western Mediterranean at this time, the hinterland was occupied by peoples living in tribal, non-urbanized, Iron Age-style cultures. The Celts occupied most of the Iberian Peninsula, Spain and Portugal and all of Gaul, modern day France, sections of Germany, and north of the Danube River and west of the Rhine River were the Germanic tribes, at this stage unknown to the Romans. They were to enjoy a rude interruption to the Germans in the second century B.C.

The situation in the west is not terribly complex. Civilized urbanized states in the Greek colonies in Sicily, an expansive naval area sphere of influence under the Phoenician colony of Carthage, stretching along the coastal regions of the western Mediterranean and then inland from those people the Romans and Greeks called barbarians, those living in non-urbanized tribal warrior-type societies. The situation in the eastern Mediterranean is completely different and requires somewhat closer attention. The eastern Mediterranean had a history of civilization that went back long before Rome was even conceived of. Many of these civilizations were as old to the Romans of the third century B.C. as the Romans are to us, if not older. Here in the east Mediterranean, we find the crucibles of civilization, Egypt going back to at least 3000 B.C. as an organized and civilized state. Even older still, in the area of Iraq, stretching its influence up into Syria, the ancient heritage of the Mesopotamians, going back to 3500 B.C. And, in Asia Minor, the very ancient history of the Hittites, going back to the Bronze Age. The Hittites were no longer around in the third century B.C., but still the heritage of civilization, the tradition of living in urbanized cultures in the east Mediterranean, indeed. Let's not forget as well the Greeks.

It is not my purpose to review the ancient history of the eastern Mediterranean in this course. Rather, we want to focus on the period or the situation as it existed around 270 B.C., which was very complex indeed. The situation in the east around 270 B.C. was a product of the conquest of one of the greatest military adventurers in human history, Alexander the Great, a Macedonian king who had conquered the extent of the Persian Empire between 334 and 323 B.C. It is a remarkable story in itself, but we don't have the time or space to deal with it in detail here. He had encountered a vast area of land that incorporated pretty much all of the Near East, Egypt, Greece, and stretching his realm as far eastward as the northern borders of India. Then, he died rather suddenly of a fever in 323 B.C., while still a young man, only 33 years old. The story goes that on his deathbed, he was asked, "To whom do you wish to leave your empire?" He responded "*kratistos*"—"To the strongest." In doing so, he sparked a 50-year cycle of civil war among his generals who competed with one another initially for control of all of Alexander's empire but eventually for control over what corners of it they could successfully defend.

When the dust had settled from these rounds of wars, three major kingdoms called the Hellenistic kingdoms, since they were inheritors of Greek culture, but were not completely Greek, which is often called the Hellenic culture, they were Hellenistic, Greek-like, since they often melded elements of the pre-Greek cultures with Greek cultures to form a Greek-ish culture that is termed Hellenistic. Three major states had emerged from the wars among Alexander's generals. In Egypt sat the Ptolemies, one of Alexander's generals had been called Ptolemy and he had grabbed Egypt for himself, and figured that that was sufficient for him and established a dynasty of Macedonian kings, Greek-style kings, who ruled over Egypt as a dynasty starting in the 330s B.C. and continuing on down to 31 B.C. In control of Egypt is the Hellenistic kingdom of the Ptolemies.

In Syria, another one of Alexander's generals, a man called Seleucus had managed to seize control of the central portion of Alexander's empire. He established a dynasty there called the Seleucid dynasty. That is, it was the dynasty of Seleucus, which was a very powerful state and in terms of territory, the largest of the Hellenistic kingdoms. Technically, the Seleucids ranked or rated their empire as starting in India and coming all the way into the Aegean Sea. So, technically, the Seleucids were the largest, a very powerful emerged kingdom, but the capital of the Seleucid Empire was at Antioch in Syria on the coast of the eastern Mediterranean. In the Macedonian homeland, the place from which Alexander had emerged to conquer so much of the eastern world was the Antigonid dynasty. This was a dynasty founded again by one of Alexander's generals. It is rather an irony that Alexander's dynasty itself was one of the first casualties of the wars following his death. None of Alexander's children or successors ever ruled any of his realms again. It was divided up among his generals. Antigonus was the man who seized control of Macedon, so his dynasty was called the Antigonid dynasty.

These are all powerful, rich, well-organized kingdoms, and it is important to stress, antagonistic toward each other. They don't feel a tremendous degree of brotherhood. After all, they have been forged in the context of civil war. So, they are continually competing with each other diplomatically and occasionally militarily over the traditional areas of dispute between these various zones in the eastern Mediterranean. For instance, the Ptolemaic dynasty in Egypt, and the Seleucid dynasty in Syria competed over the traditional zone of Palestine, which was the area that usually powers in Assyria and powers in Egypt tended to compete over. We can find hints and reflections of this competition in biblical literature, especially in the books of the Maccabees, which reflect control of Palestine by the Seleucids in the second century B.C.

Also, the Antigonids and the Seleucids were in competition with each other over Asia Minor, modern day Turkey. It must be said that although these conflicts between the major powers were shifting (they were not continuous) none of these powers gained complete supremacy over the others, and as a result, between them, independent states were given a chance to emerge. By playing the major powers off against each other, smaller independent but no less powerful states have emerged. I am not going to go over them all, but I want to focus on three areas we will be featuring in our story as we look at Roman expansion in this area.

The first area is Greece itself. The main part of Greece was technically under the influence of the Antigonids in the northern regions, but there were two leagues of independent city-states that controlled Greece. In the northern part of Greece, there was the league called the Aetolian League, and in the area of the Peloponnese there was the league called the Achaean League. These were leagues of independent city-states working together. Both leagues were mutually antagonistic, and both leagues together were antagonistic toward the Antigonids. So, you see the complexity of the situation. The complexity of the politics going on here is quite remarkable because we are dealing with an organized system of statehood that has a long heritage in the east Mediterranean. If we turn to the states we want to focus on, the independent states, besides the area of Greece, in Asia Minor, a very sophisticated highly artistically rich kingdom had emerged in the area of northwestern Turkey called Pergamum. This was the kingdom of the Aetolians in Pergamum and was a very affluent, highly sophisticated state that managed to survive in the buffer zone between the Antigonids and the Seleucids.

Finally, off the coast of Turkey was the island of Rhodes. Rhodes emerged in the Hellenistic period as a major naval power. They were a powerful trading people, but they protected their trade with a very powerful navy, and as a result, managed to defend themselves against attacks. In fact, they were often used by the Hellenistic kings in mutual conflicts as a sort of mercenary navy and so forth. So,

Rhodes managed to carve out for itself a sphere of influence in the Mediterranean. To summarize, we have the major powers of the Ptolemies in Egypt, the Seleucids in Syria and the Antigonids in Macedon. Between them we have two leagues of independent city-states in Greece, the kingdom of Pergamum in Asia Minor in modern day Turkey, and off the coast of Turkey in Rhodes, the powerful naval estate of Rhodes.

In this complex situation, this complex quilt of power and conflict, the rise of Rome in Italy was not really considered to be a major event. The western Mediterranean did not really interest the eastern powers. They were very much concerned with and focused on the Aegean Sea and their mutual conflicts with each other. The status of the west Mediterranean was not really a matter of interest to the eastern powers. So, most of the major powers of the international scene didn't pay particularly close attention to the rise of Rome as the dominant power in mainland Italy. There are two exceptions to that rule, Carthage and later on the Ptolemies of Egypt.

In our sources, Carthage is reported as having made three treaties with Rome, the first one as far back as the first year of the Roman Republic, 509 B.C. The second was in 348 B.C. and the third in 306 B.C. These are three treaties that are reported to us in our sources. The treaties are highly disputed and some scholars are skeptical especially of the first one. The say why would Carthage pay any attention to what was really then an extremely regional, extremely unimportant place. At the end of the sixth century B.C., why would they be interested in Rome at this time?

Our main source for this first treaty is Polybius who states its contents, and says that it was visible in Rome of his day. He could go and see the treaty, a copy of which was visible in one of the public buildings in Rome of his day. Other sources mention that the first treaty of Rome and Carthage was the one of 348 B.C., and there is this dispute. How many treaties were there between Rome and Carthage? When was the first one, and so on. The testimony of Polybius is very important. It is extremely difficult to discount what Polybius says. He is very reliable. He tends to be a very reliable source, and before throwing Polybius out, I think we have to have a reason. If he says that he saw a treaty between Rome and Carthage that dated to the first year of the republic, then that has to be taken seriously. One of the pieces of evidence (this is an aside, a matter of the way that evidence can sometimes be quite congruent) that turned up quite recently seemed to confirm that this was quite possible, that there was a treaty between Rome and Carthage as early as the end of the sixth century. At the town of Pergi, on the coast of Etruria, some temples were located, Etruscan temples, and in those temples were found three gold tablets which recorded various religious donations. Two of the tablets were in Etruscan and one was in Punic, the language of the Carthaginians. This would seem to suggest that the Carthaginians did have an interest in the western coast of central Italy as early as the sixth century B.C., because these tablets date to about 500 B.C. That the Romans and Carthaginians could have had a treaty as early as 500 B.C. is not unreasonable.

The thrust of all of these treaties as far as we can see was to delineate a sphere of influence. The Carthaginians agreed that they would not interfere directly on the mainland of Italy, and the Romans agreed that they would not interfere outside of the mainland of Italy. So, these are non-aggression pacts that allow you to establish spheres of influence. Here is one state, Carthage that is taking notice of the rise in Roman power. I would not be surprised if Carthaginian trading interests seem to have extended into the western seaport of Italy, it would not be surprising for Carthage to pay attention to what is going on with the rise of Rome and apparently trying to secure Roman cooperation in establishing spheres of interest.

The other major state that paid any attention to Rome's rise to power was Ptolemaic Egypt, which in 273 B.C. declared friendship with Rome. This is an important date, because it is two years after the withdrawal of Pyrrhus from Italy, so clearly the failure of Pyrrhus to defeat the Romans and carve out a little Italian empire in the southwestern portion of Italy drew the attention of the Ptolemies. Epirus and Ephesus are two of the smaller Hellenistic states that was around at the time, and it obviously drew the attention of the Ptolemies that a well organized state like Ephesus fighting in the Macedonian style had failed to beat Rome decisively. Therefore, in 273 B.C., the Ptolemies declared friendship with the Romans. We will see that this was one of the smartest things that the Ptolemies ever did. By declaring friendship with the Romans at this early stage, they avoided the military attention of the legions right down to 31 B.C., and as a result, the Ptolemaic dynasty of Egypt was the longest lived of the Hellenistic kingdoms. While the other Hellenistic kingdoms were being crushed by the legions, the Ptolemies were friends of the

Roman people and so avoided that fate at least until the first century B.C.

Even then, we will see that the ultimate fate of the Ptolemies was tied up with the workings of the Roman state and the development of the Roman revolution. All of that yet-to-come.

The situation then in the Mediterranean world prior to the emergence of Rome as a major power is a complicated one. There are many states especially in the eastern half of the Mediterranean. Many highly organized, urbanized, sophisticated states with a long heritage of civilization and independent statehood behind them, with the immediate heritage of Alexander the Great's conquest behind them, and at the time that the Romans were to emerge onto the international scene, mutually antagonistic, not successfully getting along with each other. In the western Mediterranean as we've seen there was the major mercantile power of Carthage, which we will look at in the beginning of the next lecture. If you were a betting person, if you had some drachmas or shekels to put down on a table on the wager, "Who in the next 100 years will be the major power in the Mediterranean?" and you are making this wager around 270 B.C., you would have to be especially percipient to have picked the Romans. The smart money would have been on one of the major powers of the eastern Mediterranean, the Ptolemies, perhaps the Seleucids with their vast resources drawn from Asia, or possibly, you could have chosen the power of Carthage, although that would be a rather less safe bet, since the Carthaginian interests were primarily mercantile rather than centered on the issue of power holding.

One of the reasons that you would have to be especially percipient is that the Romans in the period prior to the first Punic War were not a major naval power. If you were to control the Mediterranean Sea, you were going to need a navy. This is why the Carthaginians or any of the major powers of the east Mediterranean would be good bets, but the Romans not necessarily so. They did not have a navy of the sort for coastal defense. Naturally, if you are a land based power in Italy you will need to defend your coast in some degree, and they have fought naval battles, most notably at the end of the fourth century B.C., the Battle of Actium, which has a good story attached to it because after that battle, the Romans sawed off the ramming beaks of the enemies' ships they had captured and brought them back for almost trophies. They attached them to the speaker's platform in the

Roman Forum. The Latin word for beaks, which is what describes the large bronze ramming fronts of ancient warships, was *rostra*, meaning "the beaks". That is where we get the word rostrum for any speakers platform, it actually means beak. Strange, but that is the reason why. The Romans did have a naval capacity of sorts, but it could not in any way have matched the serious naval powers of Carthage which had extensive trading interests that stretched all the way from Spain, covered parts of Sardinia, and as we have seen showed an interest in the status of affairs on mainland Italy in the central area.

In the east Mediterranean was the powerful navy of Rhodes and the Seleucids could martial a powerful navy from their Phoenician underlings, subjects. The absence of a Roman naval power would be one of the reasons most people at the time did not pay much attention to the growth of Roman power. It would seem to have been a very regional thing. "It is going to affect the people of Italy, but we in Turkey and Syria are quite safe." How wrong they were to be. It was to be Carthage that was to make the first mistake of rousing Roman wrath and it is to the first Punic War and the titanic struggle that that involves that we will turn our attention in the next lecture.

Lecture Twelve
Carthage and the First Punic War

Scope:

Conflict with Carthage marked the beginning of Rome's rise to world power. The rise of the Roman Empire falls into two broad periods: the conquest first of the western and then of the eastern Mediterranean. We begin our survey of the first phase by outlining the development and nature of the Carthaginian state, Rome's greatest rival in the west. The course of the First Punic War is then surveyed and the ramifications of Rome's victory for both protagonists are assessed.

Outline

I. Rome's rise to dominance of the entire Mediterranean basin falls into two broad phases.

   A. First came the conflicts with Carthage that led to Rome controlling the entire western Mediterranean.

   B. The second phase was Rome's complex involvement in the affairs of the Hellenistic kingdoms to the east.

II. Carthage was an ancient Phoenician city run by a mercantile oligarchy.

   A. Carthage (located in what is modern-day Tunisia) had a long history of involvement in the western Mediterranean.

   1. By tradition, Carthage was founded in 814 B.C. by Phoenician traders.

   2. Located on a superb harbor with a fertile hinterland and endowed with an enterprising populace, the city quickly rose to a position of power.

   3. By the sixth century B.C., Carthaginian trading posts could be found all along North Africa, in western Sicily, Sardinia, Corsica and Spain.

   4. Conflict with the Greek colonies of Sicily, especially Syracuse, was frequent in the fifth and fourth centuries B.C.

   5. By the time the Romans had conquered the Italian mainland, a sort of balance of power obtained in Sicily, with Syracuse dominant in the eastern half of the island and Carthage in the west.

      6. Carthage maintained her overseas interests through diplomacy backed by a large fleet and mercenary armies.

B. Carthage was run by rich merchant families.

      1. Carthage originally had been ruled by a governor, but this autocracy had early given way to an oligarchy of ruling families.

      2. Like the Roman Republican oligarchy, two judges *(suffetes)* were elected annually, and there was a senate-like council.

      3. An unusual feature was a permanent court of 104 lifetime members, who scrutinized the affairs of professional generals and admirals.

C. Carthaginian motivation was driven by concerns of profit and cost-effectiveness, which differed greatly from Roman motivation.

      1. Carthage was run like a large company, with citizens getting a share in the profits of trade.

      2. The Carthaginians resorted to war when necessary but preferred peaceful means of resolving potential conflicts.

      3. In contrast, the Romans were motivated by the sociopolitical considerations of loyalty to one's friends and allies and maintaining face.

III. The First Punic War started small and by accident, but developed into a titanic struggle for control of Sicily.

A. The spark that ignited the First Punic war was small.

      1. Italian adventurers, called the Mamertines, seized the eastern Sicilian city of Messana and, when pressured by Syracuse, appealed first to Carthage and then to Rome.

      2. The humiliation of the Carthaginian fleet and the movement of the Romans into Sicily caused the Carthaginians to send troops to Sicily to crush the Mamertines.

      3. This affair brought Rome and Carthage into open conflict.

B. The course of the war fell into three phases.

    1. The first phase (264–60 B.C.) saw Roman and Punic armies fighting on land in Sicily. The Roman feat of arms in storming and capturing Agrigentum in 262 B.C. cowed the Carthaginians, who avoided engaging the legions in a set-piece land battle for the rest of the war.

    2. Roman frustration at the Punic ability to resupply Sicily by sea led to the second phase of the war, fought on the Tyrrhenian Sea and in Africa (260–55 B.C.).

        a. The Romans built a huge fleet in a few months and put to sea in 260 B.C., defeating the Carthaginians at the battle of Mylae.

        b. A Roman invasion of North Africa in 256 B.C. ended with the ambush and defeat of the Roman force in 255 B.C., followed shortly thereafter by the destruction of the Roman fleet in a storm off Sicily.

    3. The third and final phase of the war was fought on Sicily and the surrounding seas (255–41 B.C.).

    4. The Carthaginians fought most of this phase of the war as a guerrilla campaign from their impregnable bases at Mt. Eryx and Mt. Hercte in western Sicily. Both sides also vied for control of naval bases in Sicily.

    5. Carthaginian cost-effective thinking hampered their war effort and, in 241 B.C., when they faced a new Roman fleet at the Aegates Islands, they were roundly defeated.

C. The Romans imposed weighty terms on defeated Carthage.

    1. In 241 B.C. the Carthaginians surrendered.

    2. The Romans imposed a huge war indemnity and debarred Carthage from Sicily (which Rome promptly annexed as its first overseas province).

IV. The First Punic War had important ramifications for Rome and for Carthage.

  A. Rome enjoyed several benefits as a result of its victory in the First Punic War.

    1. The Romans had been drawn out of the Italian peninsula and now possessed their first overseas province, the fertile island of Sicily.

    2. The Romans now possessed the largest fleet in the Mediterranean.

3. They took advantage of their fleet and Punic weakness to annex Sardinia and Corsica in 238 B.C., further encroaching into the traditional Carthaginian sphere of activity.
4. Roman tenacity and determination in the face of adversity had been made clear to all.

B. Defeat drove Carthage to new pastures.
1. The closing of the seas around Sicily and Italy drove Carthage westward.
2. Between 241 and 220 B.C. the Carthaginians carved out a small empire in Spain.
3. In certain Carthaginian circles, the Roman victory was too bitter a pill to swallow and an even larger conflict was to emerge from this circumstance.

Essential Reading:

Polybius, *The Rise of the Roman Empire*, book 1.

Cary and Scullard, *A History of Rome*, chapter 12.

Supplemental Reading:

Lancel, *Carthage: A History*.

Questions to Consider:

1. What advantages did Carthage have over Rome as it entered the First Punic War?

2. How do you explain the Carthaginian failure in this conflict? Can you identify any single turning point in the war and argue why it was decisive?

Lecture Twelve—Transcript
Carthage and the First Punic War

Hello and welcome to the twelfth lecture in The History of Rome. We have now surveyed the rise of Roman power on the mainland of Italy. We have set the stage for the expansion of Rome in the east Mediterranean by looking at the national scene as it looked around 270 B.C. It is now time to turn our attention to the actual expansion of Rome in the Mediterranean, a rapid and remarkable event in the history of the world, noted by contemporaries, which we will first of all outline in the next few lectures, then seek explanations for a later lecture.

Rome's rise to dominance can broadly be divided into two halves. The first deals with the western Mediterranean, specifically the city of Carthage. In the second half, it turns its attention to the highly developed Hellenist and Hellenistic half of the eastern Mediterranean in the period beginning around 200 B.C. or so. So, if Rome's conflict with Carthage starts in 264, the first 60 years really see Rome concentrating on the western Mediterranean and then the subsequent 60 years see Rome concentrating on the eastern Mediterranean. It falls quite nicely into two chronological phases. First, we will deal with Carthage, outline the nature of the Carthaginian state, examine how it was that Rome and Carthage first came into conflict, outline the course of the war, and then discuss the ramifications for Rome and Carthage of this, the first Punic War.

Carthage by tradition was founded in 814 B.C., by the Phoenicians, although archaeology reveals nothing earlier than the mid-eighth century at the site, so that date is open to question. It was founded by the Phoenician traders whom the Romans called *Puni*, hence the name of these wars is the Punic Wars. The Romans called Carthaginians, Phoenicians *Puni*, in their language. That is why we speak about the Punic Wars, not the Carthaginian Wars. It was located on a magnificent harbor, highly recommended as a place to visit, if you ever get a chance. If you ever visit North Africa, I can recommend it highly. Carthage is located on a superb natural harbor with a fertile hinterland. When we add into the mix an enterprising population such as the Phoenicians, then the city was quickly to rise to a position of influence in the western Mediterranean.

By the sixth century B.C., the Carthaginians already had established trading posts all along the coast of North Africa to the Atlantic Ocean, as well as on Sicily, Sardinia, Corsica and Spain. Their traditional enemies in the region were the Greek colonies of Sicily, particularly Syracuse. The Carthaginians, the Syracusans and some other Greek states there fought a long series of wars for control of the island, which were still unresolved in the third century B.C. A sort of balance of power in Sicily pertained by the state with the Carthaginians, broadly speaking, in control of the western half of the island and the Greeks, especially Syracuse, in control of the eastern half of the island of Sicily. Carthage maintained her overseas interest through a mixture of diplomacy, backed by a large naval capacity and mercenary armies. This was because Carthage was run predominantly by mercantile families and interests and had a shape in terms of its government, so far as we can make it out, analogous to the Roman republic. There was an oligarchy of leading families grouped together in a senate-like council. This had evolved it appears from an earlier form of autocracy, when a king-like figure called the governor had been in control. Rather like the Roman republic the Carthaginians appear to have moved from monarchy to a sort of oligarchic system of government. These ruling families had a senate-like council. They had, every year, two leading magistrates whom they called *suffetes* who were sort of like the councils. There was also a popular assembly of adult male citizens, the function of which remains obscure to us. A very unusual feature of the Carthaginian state was a permanent standing court of 104 lifetime members whose job it was to scrutinize the activity of public officials and generals who were hired or sent out on Carthaginian business.

Rather like Darth Vader, the Carthaginians did not take well to failure by their underlings, and it was common for them to crucify generals and admirals who failed in their tasks—especially if they were deemed in this court to have been negligent in any way, or worse, if they had been taking bribes. They were tough task masters, and the officials were kept in play, on their toes, by this 104 lifetime member court of officials. Carthaginian motivation was driven by merchant-like interests of interests of profit and cost-effectiveness. This is what really drove and stimulated the Carthaginians in all of their actions. This differed considerably from Roman stimuli, Roman motivations. Carthage in some ways was run like a large company. I often describe it to my students as "Carthage Inc." They are interested in using their navy, but only to back up their trade interests. It seems that every year the profits of the state were toted up and shared among the citizens, almost like shareholders. That is a rather crude analogy, but there is some truth to it. They would resort to war when it was necessary, but if they could find a peaceful solution through diplomacy or threats, they would prefer to do that. War was costly, and that is the last thing the Carthaginians wanted to face was a costly endeavor.

In contrast, the Romans were motivated more by socio-political concerns. They were concerned to maintain loyalty with their allies. They were concerned to maintain face in the face of their allies. Cost-effectiveness was not something that featured heavily in the Roman motivational agenda. So, it was that in the middle of the third century B.C., these two states—one the land-bound state of Rome, the other, the mercantile naval-based state of Carthage faced each other now in close proximity, especially across the straits of Messina between Sicily and mainland Italy where the Romans were in control. The way that these two great states came into conflict is almost ludicrous, and it was indirect. It is worth looking at this cause of the war in some detail just to see a demonstration of how historical contingency from apparently minor incidents can lead to titanic and serious consequences.

It seems that around 288 or 289 B.C., a group of Italian adventurers from the area of Campania who call themselves "The Sons of Mars," Mamertines, were in the employ of one of the rulers of Syracuse. When this ruler died, they found themselves out of work and began marching up the eastern coast of Sicily to make their way home to southern Italy. When they reached the town of Messana, which is in the very northeastern corner of Sicily, across the straits from Rhegium on the mainland of Italy, they changed their plan. They liked the look of this place. This was a Greek city-state, and the local rulers of Messana took them in, put them up in their houses and generally treated them very well. In repayment, the Mamertines, on an agreed-upon night, cut the throats of their hosts, robbed all their possessions and their wives and seized control of the town of Messana [alternative spelling Messina]. For the next 20 or so years, they took advantage of the Syracusan and Carthaginian conflicts on Sicily, and carved out a sort of brigand kingdom in the north corner of Sicily. They even had the temerity to issue coinage as if they were a legitimate state, so they obviously had high aspirations for themselves even if they were to overlook their rather ignominious origins.

As the Greeks increasingly looked like they were coming out on top in the conflict with Carthage over Sicily, the position of the Mamertines in Messana grew increasingly more perilous. Eventually, they began to fear that the Syracusans would attack them and punish them, since most of their victims in forming their brigand kingdom had been Greeks. So, they appealed to a nearby Carthaginian fleet and commander for assistance in 266 B.C. The Carthaginian naval commander brought his ships into the harbor at Messana and took Messana under the protection of Carthage. The Syracusans who were threatening the Mamertines decided that it was not worth fighting a full-scale war against Carthage against these desperados in Messana and backed off. That would really have been that if it had not been for a strange decision on the part of the Mamertines. For whatever reason (we wish we knew why) they felt uncomfortable under the Carthaginian protection, and they appealed across the Straits of Messana to a Roman garrison on the mainland at the town of Rhegium. They used as the basis of their appeal the fact that they were Italian mainlanders, Italians like those Romans, that they worshipped the same gods, unlike those foreign Carthaginians who worshipped their own gods. "Here we are the sons of Mars." Mars, after all, was the ancestry of the Roman people. Remember he was supposed to be the father of Romulus. So, they made all these emotional appeals to the Romans, who after a heated debate in the Senate decided to accept Messana under the Mamertines into the friendship of the Roman people. The technical term is *fides,* into the faith, loyalty, area of influence of the Roman people. This was a momentous decision. It didn't seem so at the time, but it was in fact a momentous decision.

The Romans then moved a small garrison over the Messana, and the Mamertines and the Romans combined forced the Carthaginian commander to withdraw. You can imagine the reception he received when he returned to Carthage, having been judged to behave stupidly, he was crucified. The Syracusans still wanted to exact their vengeance on the Mamertines, and now they actually allied with their former enemies, the Carthaginians to attack Mamertines in Messana. Remember, now the Messanans are under the control, or at least the protection, of the Romans. This is how indirectly, when the Syracusan and Carthaginian force attacked the Messanans, the

Romans felt themselves obligated to defend their new friends. As a result Roman and Punic forces came into conflict over people who were to all intents and purposes gangsters. The conflict started in 264 B.C., and it is not my intention to go over the details of this war and all its various aspects. We will outline its course dividing it into three main phases. We will also pause on occasion to look at illustrative events that tell us the nature of the war, the enormous efforts that were expended on both sides in its prosecution, and to draw out some of the dramatic nature of this huge struggle between Carthage and Rome that lasted from 264 B.C. to 241 B.C.—the First Punic War.

The first phase of the war, the first four years from 264 B.C. to 260 B.C., was fought on land in Sicily. This is where the Carthaginians had traditionally always done their fighting, in the area of Italy, and the Romans had been drawn into Sicilian affairs via the Mamertines at Messana. The first battles took place on land over Sicily. Whatever the reason for the start of the war, whatever the Mamertines and the beginning the war, once the war started, they were forgotten. Now, it quickly evolved into a struggle between Carthage and Rome for control of Sicily. So, the original war aims were forgotten. If it was trying to restore the Mamertines, to save them, forget that. They vanished from history. Now it is fighting for control of Sicily. A rather typical feature of war is they often escalate in their goals once they have started. The salient event in this particular phase of the war is the capture by storm by the Romans of the fortified town of Agrigentum in the south coast of Sicily. I have been to this place. It is a very formidable, fortified location. It is quite amazing to think that the Romans could have taken it by direct frontal assault, but they did. In 262 B.C., they drove out the Carthaginians who were there. This was such a terrifying event for the Carthaginians that for the rest of the war they avoided any direct open battle of the legions. They figured that the Romans, if they could do that, they were not going to be easy people to beat on the field.

Despite having defeated the Carthaginians on land, the Romans quickly realized that they were going to have to develop some sort of naval capacity if they were going to win the war since Carthage could simply re-supply their force in Sicily by sea. The Romans, at this stage, were not a major naval power as we saw at the end of the last lecture. So, in 260 B.C., they built a massive fleet, from scratch. The story goes that they built it on the model of a captured

Carthaginian warship. There is reason to doubt that particular story since we have seen that the Romans did have a form of coastal defense prior to the Punic Wars, but it does make for a good story. It is sort of the first example of an arms race and military secrets on how to build a seafaring warship, to capture a Carthaginian warship and copy it. That story, however, might well be untrue. Once the Romans had built their fleet, we enter the second phase of the war that stretches from 260 B.C. to 255 B.C. It sees the Romans in their first naval engagement emerging victorious. This is the Battle of Mylae off the coast of Sicily in 260 B.C. They did this primarily by developing a technology that allowed them to transfer their land-based superiority onto the seas. They developed a mechanism called "The Raven," *corvus,* which is essentially a large bridge on a swivel that has a spike at the far end of it. While the traditional form of warfare was to ram enemy ships and sink them, the Romans would draw up along side the enemy ship, drop the bridge across. The spike would then impale itself in the deck of the enemy's vessel, tying the two together. Then the Romans would send their marines over, basically transforming their ships into platforms for land-style warfare, in which the Romans had the advantage.

So confident were the Romans now that they got carried away with themselves, and sent an invasion force into Africa in an attempt to attack Carthage directly. This invasion force left in 256 B.C., and in 255 B.C. it was completely annihilated when it was ambushed in a valley near Carthage. This year also saw an enormous reversal of Roman fortunes in a most silly fashion. The Romans, despite the fact that they had built their navy and were developing themselves as a naval power were not really accustomed to matters maritime and they had left their large fleet exposed on the western side of Sicily, when a three-day storm struck. They lost 77 percent of their fleet to a storm. To get an idea of the scale of that catastrophe, when the Japanese imperial navy attacked the U.S. Navy harbored at Pearl Harbor in 1941, the U.S. Navy lost 3 percent of its entire fleet—26 percent of its war fleet. That was considered to be an appalling catastrophe. In this storm, not even enemy action, the Romans lost 77 percent of their war fleet. This would have been enough for most states to have considered negotiating a peace, but in typical Roman fashion, they just knuckled down, and within three months, they had rebuilt their fleet.

The final phase of the war stretches from this rebuilding of the Roman fleet, 255 to 241 B.C. and illustrative of the differences between Roman and Carthaginian motivations. The Carthaginians once again focused their attentions on Sicily. They decided to conduct guerilla-style operations against Roman interests in Italy and fortified some naval bases and some land bases and sent out land-based raiding parties to harry Roman lines of communication and Roman supply lines. This particular system of warfare seemed to be going very well for the Carthaginians, and they were finding the maintenance of their navy a somewhat burdensome affair. Remember, cost-effectiveness is one of their chief forms of motivation. Maintaining a large navy that isn't to be used was really quite expensive, so, as a result, they decided that they would demobilize large sections of their navy. Between 248 and 242 B.C., while the land forces on Sicily are harrying the Roman lines of communication, the Carthaginians demobilize (disperse) much of their main naval force. In the same period the Romans built 200 new ships. The longer the war dragged on, the greater was the advantage given to the Romans. They were the ones interested in prevailing in securing political and military dominance over areas of territory. The Carthaginians were interested in counting the shekels. "How much is this costing us?" The longer the war dragged on, the less cost effective the war was from the Carthaginian perspective.

By the time the Carthaginians had realized that the Romans were now well equipped with a new navy, it was too late. They cobbled together as best they could a naval force, and sent it out to try to tackle the new Roman fleet. The two fleets met at the Aegates Islands just off the western seaboard from Sicily, and the Romans crushed the Carthaginian fleet. The Carthaginians were forced to surrender.

This was the first major overseas war that the Romans embarked upon. Its course which we have just outlined was an epic one involving major defeats and successes for both sides. The forces of the war shifting to and fro, but what shines again and again reading about this struggle, and we will be seeing it repeatedly as we look at Roman expansion across the rest of the Mediterranean, is the Roman sense of determination, their dogged stubbornness to prevail in the face of sometimes overwhelming odds. Catastrophes that would have caused other states to consider negotiating a peace merely caused the Romans to knuckle down and work harder, to redouble their efforts.

With the Carthaginians humiliated and defeated, the Romans imposed a vast war indemnity on the Carthaginian state. They hit them where it would hurt most, in their purses. They levied an indemnity of 3200 talents of silver. One talent would have made any individual a millionaire in the ancient world, and here was a war indemnity of 3200 talents. Carthage was also forced to cede all its interests in Sicily to Rome, who now adopted Sicily as its first overseas province. In 241 B.C., Sicily becomes the first province of the Roman people. The Syracusans, who had wisely decided to side with Rome, when push came to shove, were allowed to exist as an ally of the Roman people, but the rest of Sicily became a province. In the years following the first Punic War, the Carthaginians got involved in a very silly conflict in their homeland with their own army. The Carthaginians were not a citizen-based militia like the Romans. In typical Carthaginian fashion, they hired their armies, mercenary armies. Since they had lost the war against Rome, they found themselves unable to pay their mercenary armies, which parked outside the city, and they ended up having to fight them. They actually had to fight their own troops. This was a great period of turmoil for the Carthaginian state, and the Romans took full advantage of the Carthaginians being so wrapped up in fighting their own mercenary army. In 238 B.C., they seized Corsica and Sardinia, and took those two islands also as provinces of Rome. So, by 238 B.C., the Romans had extended their power outside of Italy. They were now in control of Sicily and in control of Sardinia and Corsica.

The first Punic War had major ramifications for both Rome and Carthage. In the first place, the Romans had been drawn out of the Italian peninsula for the first time. Before now, they had focused all of their attentions on gaining ascendancy over the peoples of the mainland of Italy, now they found themselves in control of territories outside of the mainland of the Italian peninsula. Secondly, and through circumstances forced on them by fighting the first Punic War, the Romans now found themselves in command of the largest navy, not just a navy, but the largest in the Mediterranean Sea. In repeated battles, they had proven themselves to be successful in using this navy, even if they had shown their greenness from time to time, especially by exposing their fleet to a three-day storm which was to destroy it in 255 B.C. That is just a sign of their neophyte nature in matters naval. By the end of the first Punic War, they were fairly adept at naval matters, and now possessed the largest fleet in the Mediterranean. It was with this fleet that they were able to annex the islands of Sardinia and Corsica in 238 B.C.

Above all, the Punic War shows us, as far as the Romans are concerned, their attitude toward conflict. They will continue to fight for as long as they can. This would have been impossible for the Romans to do were it not for their confederation of Italy as we have examined already. Were it not for the enormous resources of manpower that they could draw upon to send armies into Sicily, across to Africa, to build and man a fleet, all of that was founded in the success of Rome in organizing the Italian mainland into a confederacy. Their sheer doggedness to fight on was really a cardinal feature of Roman imperialist policy.

For the Carthaginians the defeat at the hands of the Romans was humiliating to be sure. It also had some very important ramifications. They were barred now from their traditional sphere of influence in the Mediterranean Sea. Sicily now belonged to the Romans. Roman fleets patrolled the sea between Sicily and Sardinia and Corsica. This is where we have seen the Carthaginians were most interested in this area of the sea. Now they were effectively shut out from any operations, trading or otherwise, in that area of the Mediterranean. So, they looked westward. Between 241 and 220 B.C., under a leading Carthaginian family called the Barcas, they carved out for themselves a small empire in southeastern Spain. This they did largely with mercenary armies and with naval support from their fleets which hadn't been annihilated by the Romans, but had been limited by them, and defeated by them. But, they still managed to supply an army in Spain, which over the course of the next twenty or so years, carved out quite a profitable empire for them in Spain. There were plenty of natural resources in Spain to exploit—gold mines, silver mines, lots of natural resources—and of course, very effective fighting troops in the form of Celtic troops who the Carthaginians began to take under their wing, train and form into a formidable fighting force. At 241 B.C., the end of the first Punic War and at 220 B.C., the Carthaginians, especially under the family of the Barcas, are active in Spain.

A final ramification of the first Punic War exists on a rather personal level, and I will end this lecture with a small anecdote that reveals it. In certain quarters, the defeat by Rome was considered by certain Carthaginians to be a very bitter pill to swallow. They really resented it. They especially resented Rome's seizing of Sardinia and Corsica when the Carthaginians' backs were turned trying to fight their own mercenary troops. The story goes that one Carthaginian general, a man called Hamilcar Barca, a member of the family who was busy in Spain, when he was about to set off for his command in Spain to help expand Carthaginian interests there, was (as one would do in the ancient pagan world as you were about to embark on a new endeavor,) sacrificing to the Carthaginian gods. Hamilcar had a son. The son was aged about nine or ten years. The son desperately wanted to join his daddy on the new adventures in Spain. His father said, "If you want to come with me, you must come up to the altar and take an oath with me to our ancestral gods." Hamilcar brought his son up to the altar, and forced him to swear on the ancestral gods of the Carthaginians that he would never be a friend of the Roman people. Hamilcar's son was named Hannibal, and he was to be one of the greatest banes in Roman history. In fact, he was to lead the Carthaginians to great glory in Spain, but to even further glory in Italy when, in the next lecture we will see, he invaded Italy in the course of the Second Punic War that is also quite rightfully called the Hannibalic War. That is the focus of our next lecture.

Timeline

B.C.:

c. 1200 ....Trojan War; in legend, Aeneas arrives in Italy

c. 1000..Settlement on Palatine

c. 800..Huts on Palatine and in Forum

753 ....Traditional date of the founding of Rome by Romulus and Remus

753–509 ...."Regal Period"

c. 600..Great Sewer (Cloaca Maxima) built; Forum area drained

510–509 ....Ejection of Tarquinius Superbus; establishment of Roman Republic

509–31 ...."Republican Period"

509 ....First treaty with Carthage

500–440 ....Incursions of Aequi and Volsci

494 ....First Secession of the Plebs

493 ....Treaty of Cassius between Rome and the Latins

449 ....Secession of the Plebs; Laws of the Twelve Tables published

396 ....Romans capture Etruscan city of Veii

390 ....Battle of Allia: Rome sacked by Gauls

367 ....Licinian laws; Plebeians admitted to magistracy

348 ....Treaty with Carthage renewed

343–41 ....First Samnite War

340–338 ....Revolt of Latin League

326–304 ....Second Samnite War

Glossary

(Latin terms are printed in italics and translated in either parentheses or the entry).

Acies triplex (tripartite battle formation): The set formation of the Roman Republican army when attacking.

Aediles: The aedileship originated as an office of the "Plebeian State" and became an optional magistracy in the regular *cursus honorum*; four were elected annually (six after reforms introduced under Caesar), two plebeian and two patrician (the latter termed "curule aediles"). They were in charge of the fabric of Rome, the marketplace, and public games. They had no *imperium*.

Archaeology: The study, by excavation or survey, of physical remains from the ancient world.

Augury: The practice of divination by several means, such as looking at the sky, birds, or interpreting omens.

Auspices: The reading of the gods' attitude toward a project by five means, including looking at the sky, birds, the sacred chickens feeding, or the behavior of four-legged beasts. All public business had to have favorable auspices in order to proceed. Since auspices lasted 24 hours, failure to secure favorable auspices on one day could be reversed the next.

Barbarization: Term for the growing presence and prominence of Germanic peoples in the western empire during the Late Empire.

Boni ("The Good Men"): A self-styling of the conservative senators, it denoted right-thinking, "decent" men in the senate who respected the traditional ways of doing things.

Capitecensi ("Head Count"): The lowest social class in the Roman citizen census; having no property to declare to the censors, they were counted by their heads alone, hence the name. They were grouped into a single century in the *comitia centuriata* and voted last, if they got to do so at all (since voting stopped when a majority was reached).

Censors: Two magistrates elected every five years for an eighteen-month tenure of office. They counted citizens, assigned them to their classes, reviewed the register of senators and public morals, and let contracts for tax collection and public construction. They had no *imperium*.

Clientela ("clientship"): The social system of binding high and low families together by ties of granting favors and meeting obligations. Originated in the Regal Period.

Colony: Rome started settling colonies of Latins and citizens early, as a means of securing territory. Eventually "colony" became the highest status a subject community (whether founded by Rome or not) could attain, whereby all freeborn male inhabitants became Roman citizens.

Comitia ("assembly"): Term applied to the Roman popular assemblies convened for voting on a law: the Curiate Assembly *(comitia curiata)*; Centuriate Assembly *(comitia centuriata)*; Tribal Assembly of the People *(comitia populi tributa)*; and Tribal Assembly of the Plebs *(comitia plebis tributa)* a.k.a. the Council of the Plebs *(concilium plebis)*. All voting was done in blocks as appropriate for each assembly.

Consul: Chief annually elected Republican magistrate; two elected each year; top powers in political, judicial, and military spheres. They had the greatest *imperium* in the state.

Cursus honorum ("run of offices"): Enforced order of office holding in Republican Rome, based on criteria of wealth, age, and experience. The order of ascent was quaestor (or tribune of the plebs) => aedile (optional) => praetor => consul. Ex-consuls could also become censors or dictators, and patrician ex-consuls could be elected as *interreges*.

Debt-bondage: The archaic system of ensuring cheap labor for the landowning gentry. In return for subsistence, poorer citizens became indentured servants of the landowners. One of the main issues that generated the Struggle of the Orders.

Dictator: Extraordinary magistracy instituted in crises. A dictator was appointed by a magistrate and suspended the normal government of Rome. He had no colleague but appointed an assistant called the Master of Horse *(magister equitum)*. He held office for six months or until he had completed his specific task. A dictator had the combined *imperium* of the suspended consuls and was so entitled to 24 lictors.

Dominate (< *dominus*, Latin for "master"): The term sometimes applied to the autocratic system of rule founded by Diocletian and also to the period of its operation (A.D. 284–476). The term is used chiefly to distinguish it from the Principate, as established by Augustus.

Donatism: Heresy popular in Africa in fourth and fifth centuries A.D. It disputed the right of "traitors," Christians who complied with pagan demands for the burning of Scripture during the Great Persecution (A.D. 299–311), to be full members of the Church.

Editor: One who put on gladiatorial and related spectacles at personal expense for the entertainment of the commoners.

Epigraphy: The study of inscriptions (on any surface) that derive directly from the ancient world.

Faction: Term applied to politically allied groupings in Republican senatorial politics. Applied later to the four chariot-racing teams (white, blue, green, red) and their supporters.

Fasces: Bundles of rods carried by lictors as marks of a magistrate's *imperium*. Outside Rome an ax was added to the rods to symbolize the magistrate's ability to order either corporal or capital punishment.

Fasti: Lists of annual consuls kept at Rome and other towns, usually in the forum. Later, notable events were added under their appropriate years, making surviving *fasti* (mostly from Italian towns) valuable witnesses to events.

Freedman (Latin, *libertus*): A former slave raised to the status of citizenship upon manumission but still bound to the owner as a client.

Gallia (Gaul): The Roman name for the Celtic-controlled sector of mainland Western Europe. It was divided into two parts, *Gallia Transalpina* ("Gaul across the Alps") comprising France, Belgium, and parts of Germany, the Netherlands, and Switzerland; and *Gallia Cisalpina* ("Gaul this side of the Alps"), in the Po Valley in north Italy. Both regions eventually came under Roman control.

Gens (plural, *gentes*): Normally translated as "clan," this refers to groupings of aristocratic families that seem to have their origin in the Regal Period.

Hellenism, Hellenization ("Hellas," the Greek word for "Greece"): The process whereby features of Greek culture were adopted by another culture in a variety of spheres. The Hellenization of Rome started early (sixth century B.C. at the latest) but increased in pace following direct contact with the Greek mainland in the second and third centuries B.C.

Hellenistic Period/Kingdoms: Name given to the period after Alexander the Great's death in 323 B.C.; it ended in 31 B.C., the year when Ptolemaic Egypt fell to Rome. The kingdoms into which Alexander's eastern empire divided and which existed in this period are termed "Hellenistic."

Imperial Period: Habitual designation for the period from Augustus to the "fall" in the fifth century, so covering the period 31 B.C.–A.D. 476. Usually subdivided into the Early Empire (Augustus-Nerva), the High Empire (Trajan-Severans), and the Late Empire (third–fifth centuries).

Imperium: Originally this term meant the "power of command" in a military context and was conferred on kings and, later, on consuls and praetors (and dictators). It was also used to denote the area over which the Romans had the power of command, and hence came to mean "empire" in a territorial sense.

Interpretatio Romana ("the Roman meaning"): The process in paganism of identifying newly encountered deities with established Roman divinities, such as the Punic Melqart with the Roman Hercules.

Interrex (plural, *interreges*): Extraordinary Republican magistracy elected when no consuls were in office. *Interreges* had to be patrician and held office for five days in order to conduct consular elections. They could be replaced after five days by another five-day *interrex*, this process continuing until consuls had been elected. They had no *imperium*.

Latin Rights *(ius Latii):* A half-citizenship conferred by Rome on deserving allies and colonists. Latin Rights embraced all the privileges and obligations of full citizenship minus the right to vote or stand office (though "naturalization" was possible by moving to Rome itself).

Lictors: Officials who carried the *fasces* in public as the badges of a magistrate's *imperium*. The number of lictors reflected the magistrate's relative level of *imperium*: six each for praetors (two when in Rome); twelve each for consuls; and twenty-four for dictators (but before Sulla, only twelve when in Rome).

Ludus: Any place of training or basic education, especially a gladiatorial training school.

Maiores ("elders, ancestors"): The influential and important ancestors of leading Roman families and of the state as a whole. Roman conservatism frequently looked to the *mos maiorum* ("the way of the ancestors") for examples and guidance.

Manus ("hand, authority"): An important concept in Roman domestic relations, the term denoted the authority—as represented by the hand and what was in it—wielded by fathers over their dependents, husbands over wives, owners over slaves, and so on.

Manumission ("release from authority"): The ceremony of freeing a slave.

Municipia ("township"): This technical term fluctuated in meaning over the centuries but basically described a township under Roman rule in which the freeborn inhabitants had Latin Rights or, later, full citizenship. Eventually it came to denote any self-ruling Italian community, and many provincial ones as well, that was not a citizen colony.

Mystery cults/religions: Predominantly eastern cults in which a select group of initiates went through secret rites about which they were sworn to secrecy (hence the "mystery") and thereby entered into a special relationship with the deity concerned (e.g., Mithras, Isis). A major rival to Christianity, such cults became very popular in the west in the second and third centuries A.D.

Names, Roman: The full citizen's name usually had three elements: the *praenomen* (identifying the individual; very few were in general use), the *nomen* (identifying the "clan"), and the *cognomen* (identifying a family within a clan). Extra names (usually heritable) could be accumulated through adoption or as honorific titles, or as nicknames.

Oligarchy: "Rule by a few" selected usually on the basis of birth (aristocracy) or wealth (plutocracy) or a combination of the two. From the Greek *oligos* ("few") and *arche* ("leadership").

Optimates ("The Excellent Men"): Term applied initially to broadly conservative senators who favored the traditional role of the senate at the state's helm. Eventually, it applied especially to die-hard conservatives, who opposed each and every departure from traditional procedure.

Order (*ordo*, the Latin word for "rank"): The term applied to the various social classes of citizens organized by status. Over the long course of Roman history five Orders appeared: Patrician, Plebeian, Senatorial, Equestrian, and Decurional.

Pax deorum: Term used to describe the desirable *modus vivendi* between gods and humans, it was maintained by proper ritual observance.

Paterfamilias ("father of the family"): The legal head of the Roman family, he was the eldest living male and wielded *patria potestas* ("the fatherly power") over all who lived under his roof.

Pontifex Maximus: chief priest of pagan Rome.

Populares ("Men of the People"): Term applied to (usually young) politicians who followed the lead of Ti. and C. Gracchus and employed the tribunate and plebeian assembly to implement their political agenda. *Populares*, therefore, drummed up support by backing "popular" measures (land distributions, cheap or free grain, debt relief, etc.) and tended to adopt a strongly anti-senate posture.

Praetor: Second highest annually elected Republican magistracy. Originally assistants to the consuls, six were elected each year by 150 B.C., with two more added by Sulla. They carried out judicial, political, and military functions. They had *imperium*, but lesser than that of the consuls.

Praetorian Guard/Prefect: Originally a special detachment of soldiers who guarded the CO's tent *(praetorium)* in an army camp, the term was adopted for the imperial guard of the emperor in Rome. Formed by Augustus and discreetly billeted in towns around Rome, they were barracked in a single camp on the outskirts of the city by Tiberius in A.D. 23. They numbered from 9,000–16,000 men, depending on the emperors' inclination. They played some role in imperial politics (it has often been exaggerated), killing some emperors (e.g., Gaius [Caligula]), elevating others (e.g., Claudius, Otho and Didius Julianus). Their commander, a prefect of Equestrian status, could be a person of great influence, as was the case with Sejanus under Tiberius or Macrinus, who himself became emperor in A.D. 217–218. They were disbanded by Constantine in A.D. 312.

Principate: Term used to describe both the imperial system established by Augustus and the period of its operation (27 B.C.–ca. A.D. 284).

Prodigia: Unasked-for signs from the gods, usually in the form of extraordinary or supernatural occurrences.

Publicani (literally "public men"): Term used to denote companies of (usually) equestrian members who purchased public contracts let by the censors. The most powerful were the tax collectors, who competed for contracts for particular regions, thus leaving those regions open to widespread abuse and extortion.

Quaestor: Most junior magistracy in the *cursus honorum*, ten were elected annually. They had financial duties and no *imperium*.

Regal Period: The period when kings ruled Rome, traditionally dated 753–509 B.C.

Republican Period: Traditionally dated 509–31 B.C., this long period of oligarchic rule by senate and magistrates is often subdivided into the Early Republic (down to 264 B.C. and the First Punic War), Middle Republic (264–133 B.C.), and the Late Republic (corresponding to the Roman Revolution, 133–31 B.C.).

Romanization: Modern historians' term for the process of making previously uncivilized regions into Roman ones (although it can be applied also to the adaptation of urbanized cultures to the Roman way).

Senate: Council of Roman aristocratic advisors, first to the kings, then to the magistrates of the Roman Republic, and finally to the Emperors. Its origins are obscure.

Senatus consultum (ultimum) ("[final] decree of the senate"): Advice issued by the senate to magistrates; it was not legally binding. The "final" *(ultimum)* decree was essentially a declaration of martial law first issued in 121 B.C. amid the disturbances surrounding C. Gracchus' attempt for a third tribunate and the last was issued when Caesar invaded Italy in January 49 B.C.

Tribe: A grouping of Roman citizens defined by locality (like a parish or county). There were originally only three tribes (hence the name, derived from the Latin *tres*, meaning "three"), but the number of tribes increased with Roman expansion and was eventually set at 35 (4 urban, 31 rural).

Tribune of the Plebs: Not technically a magistrate, this was the officer attached to the Tribal Assembly of the Plebs; his title derives from the tribal organization of this assembly. He had to be plebeian, was sacrosanct and could not be harmed while in office, was entrusted with looking after the interests of the plebs and could convene discussion sessions *(contiones)* or voting sessions *(comitiae)* of the plebs. His most important power was a veto on meetings of all assemblies and the Senate and on all legislation.

Triumvirate: Latinate term applied to any board of three men empowered to carry out some task (e.g., Ti. Gracchus' land commission). Usually applied (technically incorrectly) to the pact between Crassus, Pompey and Caesar formed in 60 B.C. (the so-called First Triumvirate). The Second Triumvirate comprised of Octavian, Antony and Lepidus and was legally instituted in 43 B.C.

Venatio ("the hunt"): Wild beast hunt and/or animal fights that constituted the first installment of the developed gladiatorial spectacle.

Biographical Notes

These notes are divided into two groups: (A) ancient authors and (B) historical figures. Note that these two categories are *not* mutually exclusive.

All names are listed by the form used in common English currency (e.g., "Pompey" for "Pompeius") and by whatever name they are best known ("Caesar" for "Gaius Julius Caesar," "Tiberius" for "Tiberius Julius Caesar Augustus").

A. Main Ancient Authors

Cassius Dio (ca. A.D. 164–230). Lucius Cassius Dio was a Greek senator from Asia Minor who composed an eighty-book history of Rome, of which all survives, in full or summary ("epitome") form. More useful for Imperial than Republican history, Dio is especially illuminating when addressing contemporary events under the Severans.

Cicero (3 January 106–7 December 43 B.C.). Marcus Tullius Cicero, a "new man" from Arpinum, was a moderately successful politician but a master craftsman of Latin prose. His huge corpus of surviving writings includes letters, treatises, and speeches. All are historical sources of unparalleled usefulness.

Dionysius of Halicarnassus (flourished c. 30–10 B.C.). A teacher of rhetoric who arrived in Rome at the beginning of Augustus' reign and published his twenty-book *Roman Antiquities* about twenty years later. The work covered Roman history from earliest times to the outbreak of the First Punic War, and the first eleven books have survived intact (taking the story down to 441 B.C.), with fragments of the rest also known. As such, Dionysius' work is a valuable resource for the early history of Rome. Rather like Livy, however, Dionysius' work often reads like a eulogy of Roman virtues, as manifested among "the ancestors" ("*maiores*").

Livy (59 B.C.–A.D. 17). Titus Livius hailed from Patavium in Cisalpine Gaul and benefited from the explosion of literary culture in Augustan Rome. He composed a 142-book history of Rome called "From the City's Founding" *(Ab Urbe Condita),* of which all but two books survive in full or summary form (the so-called *Periochae*). Taking Rome's history to 9 B.C., Livy's history is marred by overt moralization and patriotism.

Plutarch (c. A.D. 50–c. A.D. 120). L. Mestrius Plutarchus is an excellent example of the truly Greco-Roman culture that the Romans forged in the Imperial period. Born and raised in Chaeronea in central Greece, he traveled widely in the empire (including to Egypt and Rome) but lived most of his life in Greece. Yet he considered himself "Roman." His voluminous writings include his very useful series of "Parallel Lives" of famous Greek and Roman historical figures. He also wrote rhetorical and philosophical treatises, dialogues, and antiquarian investigations ("Greek Questions" and "Roman Questions"), mostly of a religious bent (Plutarch spent his last thirty years as a priest at Delphi in Greece). His biographies of major Romans, however, constitute his most useful contributions to this course

Polybius (ca. 200–118 B.C.). Polybius, son of Lycortas, was a prominent Greek politician in the Achaean League who, after Pydna in 168 B.C., was denounced to the Romans and interned as a hostage in Italy. Here, he was befriended by the Scipiones and wrote forty books of *Histories* to document and explain Rome's rapid rise to world dominion. Only five books survive intact, most others are known from excerpts, fragments, and summaries. Polybius, our earliest extant source for Roman history, provides a unique outsider's view on the Middle Republic and, as such, can be used with great profit.

Suetonius (ca. A.D. 70–130). Gaius Suetonius Tranquillus hailed from an Equestrian background, probably from North Africa. He was a friend of Pliny the Younger and became a secretary in the imperial service of Hadrian, but was fired in ca. 120. Among other things, he wrote biographies of the "Twelve Caesars" (Julius Caesar–Domitian) that are racy and entertaining to read but not the most reliable as historical sources.

Tacitus (ca. A.D. 56–120). So little is known of Cornelius Tacitus' life that his *praenomen* is not recoverable with any certainty (it may have been Publius or Gaius). He had a successful senatorial career under the tyrant Domitian and reached the governorship of Asia under Trajan. He wrote several monographs, but his masterpiece was the *Annals*, covering the reigns of the Julio-Claudian emperors; he also wrote the *Histories*, describing the civil wars of A.D. 69 and the Flavian dynasty. Neither work survives intact. Tacitus wrote in a clipped, acerbic style and, possessed of an acute intelligence and

Republican inclinations, presents a dark and gloomy picture of life under the emperors.

B. Historical Figures

Aeneas: Legendary sole survivor of Troy who traveled the Mediterranean and founded a line of kings at Lavinium in Latium. From this line sprung Romulus and Remus, who founded the city of Rome.

Agrippa (c. 63–12 B.C.). Marcus Vispanius Agrippa, of obscure birth, was an adherent and lifelong friend of Augustus. He joined Octavian at the very outset of his career, orchestrated the victory at Actium, and undertook several important military commands on behalf of Augustus. From 23 B.C. onwards, he was Augustus' chosen successor, married to the emperor's daughter and, from 18 B.C. until his death in 12 B.C., virtually co-emperor with Augustus. He had five children by Julia, and all three of his sons (Gaius Caesar, Lucius Caesar, and Agrippa Postumus) were adopted by Augustus as his own at various stages.

Alaric (A.D.?–410). King of the Visigoths, ca. A.D. 395–410, he embarked on a series of annual incursions first into the Balkans and then, when bought off and facing serious resistance, into Italy. Made "Master of the Soldiers" in A.D. 409, he sacked Rome in A.D. 410 and died shortly afterward.

Antony, Mark (83–30 B.C.). Marcus Antonius, of distinguished birth, fought under Caesar in Gaul and became an ardent and trusted supporter. As a close friend of Caesar's and consul in 44 B.C., he expected death with his patron but was spared. He then orchestrated the expulsion of the Liberators, snubbed Octavian, fought against him, and then joined him and Lepidus to form the Second Triumvirate in 43 B.C. As Triumvir he went east where he inherited Caesar's affair with Cleopatra VII of Egypt, fought the Parthians and saw Octavian consolidate his hold on the west. In the final conflict at Actium in 31 B.C., Antony was defeated and, with his armies defecting en masse to Octavian, he committed suicide in August 30 B.C.

Augustus (23 September 63 B.C.–19 August A.D. 14). Arguably the single most important and influential man in Roman history, he was born Gaius Octavius, of humble stock. His great-uncle, however, was Julius Caesar, in whose will he was adopted in 44 B.C. Despite being unknown and inexperienced, Octavius, now Gaius Julius Caesar Octavianus (Octavian), embarked on a bold and dangerous political career that showed daring and ruthlessness in equal measure. Along with Antony and Lepidus, he became a member of the Second Triumvirate, a legally instituted board of military dictators, and competed with Mark Antony and the Liberators for the leadership of the Roman world. By 31 B.C. he had secured this goal and, renamed Imperator Caesar Augustus in 27 B.C., he became Rome's first emperor, ushering in the Imperial Age and establishing the Principate, which remained the institutional and administrative basis for the Roman Empire for 300 years. He died peacefully at a villa in Nola on the 19th day of the month that now bore his name.

Aurelian (A.D. 215–75). Lucius Domitius Aurelianus, one of the Illyrian "Soldier-Emperors" (A.D. 270–75) was a man of great energy. He threw back barbarian invasions, initiated the construction of the massive circuit of walls still to be seen at Rome today, and reunited the divided empire. Defeating, in turn, the eastern threat of Palmyra and the western secessionist state *Imperium Galliarum*, he brought the empire under one ruler again. He was murdered by some of his officers who erroneously believed he had marked them for death.

Brutus (1; sixth century B.C.). **Lucius Junius** Brutus reputedly led the coup d'etat against Rome's last king, Tarquinius Superbus; he was one of the Republic's first two consuls. Many exemplary stories surround him, making the historical Brutus hard to discern.

Brutus (2; ca. 85–42 B.C.). **Marcus Junius** Brutus was a descendant of the previous entry. He made a show of defending Republican values against both Pompey and Caesar while courting them both. He sided with Pompey in 49 B.C. and, spared after Pharsalus, benefited greatly under Caesar's *dominatio*: he was governor of Cisalpine Gaul, 47–45 B.C., praetor in 44 B.C., and designated consul for 41 B.C. Despite these signs of Caesar's favor, Brutus joined the conspiracy against Caesar and became, along with Cassius, a leader of the Liberators. He committed suicide after the defeats at Philippi.

Caesar (100 B.C.–15 March 44 B.C.). Gaius Julius Caesar was born into an ancient but eclipsed patrician family. Possessed of astonishing intellectual talents and great charisma, his early career was bankrolled by Crassus but was not markedly revolutionary. That changed in 60 B.C. when he joined Pompey and Crassus to form the so-called First Triumvirate, an informal pact between the three to act together. His consulship of 59 B.C. was marred by massive operations of violence and intimidation. From 58–49 B.C. he conquered all of Gaul for Rome. During this time the Triumvirate broke apart, and Pompey and Caesar were left to fight it out. An enormous civil war (49–45 B.C.) saw Caesar victorious on all fronts. Ensconced in the dictatorship and displaying no tact in the exercise of power, Caesar died at the hands of a conspiracy of noblemen calling themselves "The Liberators."

Cato the Censor (234–139 B.C.). Marcus **Porcius Cato** "Censorinus" was an eminent statesman and stalwart traditionalist who, in his public posture at least, championed old Roman ways against Greek influence. His familiarity with the Greek language and detailed knowledge of its literature suggest otherwise.

Claudius (10 B.C.–A.D. 54). Tiberius Claudius Nero Germanicus was the third Julio-Claudian emperor (A.D. 41–54). Shunned by his family due to his physical defects, he devoted his youth to study and scholarship. When his nephew Gaius (Caligula) was murdered, Claudius was reputedly found by soldiers in the palace and declared emperor on the spot. The story may mask a more complex and intriguing reality. His reign was largely successful; he added Britain to the empire, ruled conscientiously, and tried to act moderately. Senatorial opposition, however, was strong and he was forced to rely increasingly on freedmen from his own house for administrative support. He was poisoned by his niece and fourth wife, Agrippina the Younger, in A.D. 54 so that her son, Nero, could succeed to the throne.

Constantine the Great (c. A.D. 272–337). Flavius Valerius Constantinus was the son of Tetrarch Constantius I. When his father died at York in Britain in A.D. 306, Constantine was hailed as emperor, contrary to the stipulations of the Tetrarchy. From then until A.D. 324, Constantine worked to establish his sole rule over the whole empire. As emperor he consolidated on Diocletian's restabilization of the empire, founded an eastern capital at Constantinople, thereby paving the way for the final division of the empire into eastern and western halves. His most lasting legacy, however, was in the area of religion, where he decriminalized and then favored Christianity. By intervening in doctrinal disputes, he laid the foundations of Catholicism by insisting on an orthodox dogma that all Christians had to adhere to. He died peacefully near Nicomedia, being baptized shortly before the end.

Diocletian (A.D. 240s–312). Gaius Aurelius Valerius Diocletianus was of obscure origins but became one of Rome's most important emperors. Coming to power in civil war in A.D. 284, he set about building on the work of his predecessors who had reintegrated the empire. Diocletian's reign, therefore, was one of consolidation. He introduced a mass of reforms in the imperial administration and bureaucracy, court protocol, and military organization that laid the basis of Late Imperial Rome. His religious policy was one of divine legitimation of imperial authority by Jupiter and Hercules, thereby setting him at odds with the Christians. The "Great Persecution" (A.D. 299–311) initiated under his rule was the closest pagan Rome came to a systematic elimination of Christianity, and even it was regional and sporadic. Having established the Tetrarchic system of succession, he was the first and only emperor to retire voluntarily in A.D. 305, only to see his clever succession scheme fall apart around him.

Gaius (Caligula) (A.D. 12–41). Son of Germanicus Caesar, the adopted son of Tiberius, Gaius (nicknamed *Caligula* "Little Boot" by the legions as a child) became emperor in March A.D. 37. Despite having no experience of administration or military affairs, he was invested with all the powers of the Principate by a fawning senate. His rule was disastrous and may have been marked by insanity (though the ancient evidence for sheer mania is not reliable). As the emperor's behavior became increasingly unacceptable, a conspiracy of Praetorian Guardsmen orchestrated his murder on 24 January A.D. 41.

Gracchi. The brothers whose careers as tribunes of the plebs mark the beginning of the Roman Revolution. Tiberius Sempronius Gracchus (ca 170–133 B.C.; tribune 133 B.C.) tackled land reform and employed uncustomary methods to get his measures passed and implemented. He was murdered along with 300 followers in a senatorial-led riot while holding an election meeting for a planned second tribunate. His brother, Gaius Sempronius Gracchus (c. 160–122 B.C.; tribune 123, 122 B.C.) implemented a more overtly anti-senatorial slate of legislation. He backed enfranchisement of the Italian allies but thereby undermined his popularity at Rome. Amid growing tensions he died in vicious street fighting in 121 B.C., along with 3,000 of his followers.

Hadrian (A.D. 76–138). Publius Aelius Hadrianus, the second of the Adoptive Emperors (A.D. 117–138), was an eccentric who traveled to every part of the empire during his reign. His accession appears to have been orchestrated by Trajan's wife, Plotina. He reversed Trajan's bellicose policies and speeded up a consolidation of the frontiers made manifest in his famous wall in northern Britain.

Hannibal (247–182 B.C.): Punic general who almost destroyed Rome in the Second Punic War. Having commanded Carthaginian forces in Spain in 221–219 B.C., Hannibal invaded Italy in 218 and inflicted three crushing defeats on the Romans at Trebia, Trasimene, and Cannae. Defeated at Zama in North Africa in 202 B.C., he was hounded by the Romans until he committed suicide in 182 B.C.

Lepidus (?–12 B.C.). Marcus Aemilius Lepidus stemmed from a respected noble house. He was a supporter of Caesar's in Spain during the civil war and his Master of Horse in 46–44 B.C. Following Caesar's murder, he allied with Antony and, as governor of Gallia Transalpina, reinforced Antony in his flight from Mutina. He formed the Second Triumvirate with Octavian and Antony in 43 B.C. Outstripped in ambition and ruthlessness by his colleagues, he was sidelined in Africa and, after a show of force against Octavian in Sicily in 36 B.C., he was stripped of his powers and housed in Circeii, near Rome. He died there in 12 B.C.

Marius (c. 157–86 B.C.). Gaius Marius, a "new man" from Arpinum, was catapulted to prominence by his successful resolution of military crises. Between 107–100 B.C. he held six consulships, in open contravention of both tradition and law. He also reformed the army in various ways, particularly in enlisting as a matter of course the Head Count and equipping them at state expense. After a disastrous sixth consulship in 100 B.C., Marius retired to private life but emerged again to take command of the Roman forces in the northern theater of the Social War (91–88 B.C.). His ensuing conflict with Sulla ended with his taking up a seventh consulship (86 B.C.), but he died a few days into it.

Nero (A.D. 37–68). Born L. Domitius Ahenobarbus, he became Nero Claudius Caesar on his adoption by Claudius in A.D. 52. His mother, Agrippina, was the sister of Gaius (Caligula) and wife of Claudius and one of the most powerful women in Roman history. Nero came to power at age 16 and proved disastrous as emperor. He devoted his time to poetry and the arts, paying little attention to administration. He was paranoid about rivals to his position and murdered most potential successors or anyone who threatened his position, including Agrippina herself in A.D. 59. He survived a major conspiracy in A.D. 65 only to fall to an army revolt in A.D. 68. He committed suicide while on the run, reduced to the status of a "public enemy."

Pompey (106–48 B.C.). Gnaeus Pompeius Magnus, the political ally and then archrival of Julius Caesar, was born of a prominent Picene family and entered Roman politics as an upstart supporter of Sulla in 83 B.C. Successful in military matters, most spectacularly against the pirates in 66 B.C., he became a popular hero. He formed the First Triumvirate with Caesar and Crassus in 60 B.C., but thereafter relations with Caesar deteriorated until civil war erupted in 49 B.C. Now posing as the champion of the Republic against Caesarian tyranny, Pompey met defeat at Pharsalus in 48 B.C. and, on fleeing to Egypt, was ignominiously decapitated by a claimant to the Ptolemaic throne in that year.

Romulus and Remus: Legendary brothers and descendants of Aeneas who founded Rome in 753 B.C. Romulus killed Remus over an argument about the size of Rome, and ascended into heaven when he died.

Romulus Augustulus (emperor, A.D. 475–476). Neither the birth nor death date of this figure is known but he may have survived into the sixth century. As a boy, he was the last emperor of the western Roman Empire, deposed by the German Odoacer in A.D. 476. His name, ironically, echoes both the founder of Rome (Romulus) and the founder of the rule of emperors (Augustus). His overthrow marks the traditional date of the "Fall of the Roman Empire."

Scipio Africanus (236–183 B.C.). Publius Cornelius Scipio Africanus was an eminent figure in the Scipionic family. He rose to prominence leading Roman armies to victory over the Carthaginians in Spain and defeated Hannibal at Zama in 202 B.C. He was involved in subsequent Roman campaigns in Spain and the eastern Mediterranean.

Septimius Severus (A.D. 145–211). Lucius Septimius Severus, of a prominent North African family, founded the Severan Dynasty (A.D.

193–235) after coming to power in civil war. As an army man, he was blunt and direct and crafted a new and more openly militaristic version of the emperorship. He fought campaigns against the Parthians, capturing their capital in A.D. 198. He died at York while on campaign in Britain in A.D. 211.

Severus Alexander (c. A.D. 209–235). Marcus Aurelius Severus Alexander, the last of the Severan Dynasty, ruled as a front for his mother, Julia Mamaea. Facing mounting general disorder and the emergence of Germanic confederations in the north and Sassanid Persia in the east, Severus spent his last years on campaign against both threats. He was murdered along with his mother by his own troops at Mainz in Germany. His death heralded a half-century of disorder and mayhem.

Sulla (c. 138–78 B.C.). Lucius Cornelius Sulla "Felix" was a scion of a patrician house fallen on hard times. He emerged as an officer under Marius in the Jugurthine and Germanic wars, 107–100 B.C. He made a name for himself commanding Roman forces in the southern theater in the Social War (91–88 B.C.) and was rewarded with the consulship of 88 B.C. Notorious for turning his armies against his political opponents, being the first to institute proscriptions, and reviving an enhanced version of the dictatorship to reform the state along conservative lines.

Theodosius the Great (c. A.D. 346–935). Theodosius was the last truly strong emperor of Rome (A.D. 379–395), and the last emperor of a united empire. He settled large numbers of Goths in the empire and made treaties with Persia. Ruling out of Constantinople, he spent some years in the west on campaign and visited Rome in A.D. 389. As a devoted Christian, he issued edicts of intolerance against paganism and would not countenance heresy. When he died, he divided the empire into eastern and western halves in his will, assigning his sons Arcadius and Honorius to rule each half respectively.

Tiberius (39 B.C.–A.D. 37). Tiberius Claudius Nero, later Tiberius Julius Caesar Augustus, was the second emperor of Rome (A.D. 14–37) and the first of the Julio-Claudian dynasty. Stepson of Augustus, he was not much liked by his stepfather but, due to the vicissitudes of fortune, ascended to the throne in A.D. 14 as Augustus' adopted son. His reign was partly successful but marred by some dreadful periods of tyranny, notably that following the fall of Sejanus in A.D. 31–33. A manic-depressive, Tiberius retired to Capri in A.D. 26 and never returned to Rome, leaving the administration of the empire to the senate and his other subordinates.

Tarquinius Superbus. The last king of Rome. He was expelled in a coup in 509 B.C. but made several attempts to regain the city. He died, unsuccessful, at Cumae in 495 B.C.

Trajan (ca A.D. 53–117). Marcus Ulpius Traianus was the first of the Adoptive Emperors (A.D. 98–117). Governor of Germany, he was adopted by the wavering Nerva in the face of army grumblings. He was a conscientious emperor, tolerant, unassuming, and even-handed. He conducted major campaigns in Dacia (A.D. 101–2, 105–6) and in the east, and added four new provinces to the empire (Dacia, Armenia, Arabia, Mesopotamia). He died of fever returning from his campaigns in the east.

Bibliography

* Denotes essential reading

Ancient Works (all references are to English translations in the Penguin Classics series, unless otherwise indicated):

*Appian, *The Civil Wars*

*Apuleius, *The Golden Ass* (Oxford World's Classics edition, translated by P.G. Walsh, 1994)

*Augustus, *Res Gestae Divi Augusi* (Oxford edition, edited by P. A. Brunt and J. M. Moore, 1967)

*Caesar, *The Conquest of Gaul, The Civil War*

*Cicero, various works. The Penguins Classics feature:

- *On Government* (extracts from several works)
- *Letters to Atticus* (complete translation)
- *Murder Trials* (four complete forensic speeches)
- *Selected Letters* (parts of *Letters to Friends*)
- *Cicero's Letters to Atticus* (the complete correspondence)
- *Selected Political Speeches* (seven speeches)

*Dio, *Roman History*. The Penguins Classics feature:

- *The Reign of Augustus* (books 50–56 of the original work)

*The *Historia Augusta* (Augustan History). The Penguin Classics feature:

- *Lives of the Later Caesars*, vol. 1 (Hadrian–Heliogabalus)

The other HA biographies (Severus Alexander–Numerian) are available in the Loeb Classical Library series published by Harvard University Press.

*Livy, *The History of Rome from its Foundation*. The Penguin Classics feature:

- *The Early History of Rome* (books 1–5)
- *Rome and Italy* (books 6–10)
- *The War with Hannibal* (books 21–30)
- *Rome and the Mediterranean* (books 31–55)

*Plutarch, *Parallel Lives*. The Penguin Classics feature:

- *Makers of Rome*
- *The Fall of the Roman Republic*

*Polybius, *The Rise of the Roman Empire*

*Sallust, *Jugurthine War and Conspiracy of Catiline*

*Suetonius, *The Twelve Caesars* (Caesar–Domitian)

J. A. Shelton, *As the Romans Did: A Sourcebook in Roman Social History*, 2nd edition (Oxford, 1998). An invaluable collection of translated excerpts from authors, inscriptions, papyri and coins assembled under thematic headings.

*Tacitus, *The Annals of Imperial Rome*, *The Histories*

Modern Works:

General:

The Cambridge Ancient History, volumes 7–12. A detailed account of Roman history, in the form of chapters written by eminent (mostly English) scholars in their respective areas of expertise.

G. Alföldy, *The Social History of Rome*, 2nd edition (Baltimore, 1988). Excellent survey of the subject infused with many perceptive insights.

E. H. Carr, *What is History?* 2nd edition (London, 1986). The idea of history perceptively discussed.

*M. Cary and H. H. Scullard, *A History of Rome Down to the Reign of Constantine*, 3rd edition (New York, 1979). A standard and respected survey of the subject, if a little dry and dense.

*M. Crawford (ed.), *Sources for Ancient History* (Cambridge, 1983). Eminent historians outline the relative merits of literary, epigraphic, and archaeological evidence.

M. I. Finley, *Ancient History: Evidence and Models* (New York, 1985). The methodology of ancient history subjected to a sometimes searing analysis.

S. Hornblower and A. Spawforth (eds.), *The Oxford Classical Dictionary*, 3rd edition (Oxford, 1996). The best reference book for classical antiquity in English.

M. Grant, *A History of Rome* (New York, 1976). A succinct account of the main events.

R. Jenkyns (ed.), *The Legacy of Rome: A New Appraisal* (Oxford, 1992). A recent assessment of the heritage of Rome to the modern world in specific fields.

L. Keppie, *Understanding Roman Inscriptions* (Baltimore, 1991). A readable survey of Latin inscriptions in their various forms.

*H. H. Scullard, *From the Gracchi to Nero* , 5th edition (London, 1982). An excellent and lucid overview of the period covered.

Early Rome and the Etruscans:

A. Alföldi, *Early Rome and the Latins* (Ann Arbor, 1965). Interesting and learned assessment of the early period of Rome's history.

G. Barker, *The Etruscans* (Malden, Mass, 1998). A recent and thorough analysis; particularly strong on the archaeological evidence.

*T. J. Cornell, *The Beginnings of Rome* (New York, 1995). Eminently readable, thorough, and stimulating account of Roman history from pre-Roman Italy to 264 B.C. Especially valuable for its summary of otherwise obscure Italian archaeological discoveries.

R. M. Ogilvie, *Early Rome and the Etruscans* (London, 1976). A now-classic assessment of early Roman history.

E. T. Salmon, *The Making of Roman Italy* (London, 1982). Emphasizes the unity of Italy under Roman suzerainty.

H. H. Scullard, *The Etruscan Cities and Rome* (London, 1971). It's all in the title.

A. N. Sherwin-White, *The Roman Citizenship*, 2nd edition (Oxford, 1973). Thorough study of the subject, with some useful observations on the early sharing of citizenship in Latium and the origins of the Roman Confederation in Italy

C. J. Smith, *Early Rome and Latium: Economy and Society, c. 1000 to 500 B.C.* (Oxford, 1996). An excellent illustration of how archaeology can be used to throw light on this early period.

Rise of the Roman Empire and Governing the Republic:

P. A. Brunt, *Italian Manpower, 225 B.C.–A.D. 14* (Oxford, 1971). Sustained critique of Toynbee's *Hannibal's Legacy.*

T. J. Cornell, B. Rankov, and P. Sabin (eds.), *The Second Punic War: A Reappraisal* (London, 1996). A stimulating and insightful series of essays by leading scholars on disputed aspects of this dramatic struggle.

P. Green, *Alexander to Actium: The Historical Evolution of the Hellenistic Age* (Berkeley, 1990). Thorough treatment of the subject, sometimes overwhelming in its scope.

—————, *Hellenistic History and Culture* (Berkeley, 1993). A more focused treatment than his *Alexander to Actium.*

W. V. Harris, *War and Imperialism in Republican Rome, 327–70 B.C.* (Oxford, 1979). Brilliantly argued critique of "defensive imperialism."

L. Keppie, *The Making of the Roman Army: From Republic to Empire*, revised edition (London, 1998). A lucid account of the development of the Roman army from earliest times to the Early Empire.

J. F. Lazenby, *The First Punic War* (Stanford, 1996). This, the first thorough treatment in English of this landmark conflict, documents the war's military operations in considerable detail.

S. Lancel, *Carthage: A History* (Oxford, 1995). Thoroughgoing account of Carthaginian history that embraces the Phoenician background; the archaeology of the site of Carthage; the political, military, cultural and artistic life of the ancient city; and its legacy to the modern world.

—————, *Hannibal* (Oxford, 1998). Recent and detailed account of Hannibal's life and campaigns.

F. Millar, *The Crowd in Rome in the Late Republic* (Ann Arbor, 1998). A clever but ultimately unconvincing attempt to argue that the Roman Republic was more democratic than has been generally thought.

K. Raaflaub, "Born to be Wolves? Origins of Roman Imperialism," in R. W. Wallace and E. M. Harris, eds., *Transition to Empire: Essays in Greco-Roman History* (London, 1996), 273–314. A concise exposition of the "systems analysis" approach to explaining Roman imperialism.

R. Stewart, *Public Office in Early Rome: Ritual Procedure and Political Practice* (Ann Arbor, 1998). A look at the evolution of office-holding in the early Roman Republic with an emphasis on the lot and the ritualistic nature of magisterial duties.

L. R. Taylor, *Roman Voting Assemblies from the Hannibalic War to the Dictatorship of Caesar* (Ann Arbor, 1966). A classic and lucid account of the subject that throws much light on the workings of the Roman Republic.

A. J. Toynbee, *Hannibal's Legacy: The Hannibalic War's Effects on Roman Life* (Oxford, 1965). A classic study arguing that the Second Punic War was the central catalyst for subsequent events in Roman history.

The Roman Revolution:

M. Beard and M. Crawford, *Rome in the Late Republic* (Ithaca, 1985). Introductory thematic survey to the society, culture, and politics of the period.

P. A. Brunt, *Social Conflict in the Roman Republic* (London, 1971). Concise survey of the issues that stimulated the Struggle of the Orders and the Roman Revolution.

T. F. Carney, *A Biography of C. Marius* (Chicago 1970). Remarkably, this short book is the only full-scale modern assessment of Marius' career in English.

D. C. Earl, *Tiberius Gracchus: A Study in Politics* (Brussels, 1963). Short, sober, and lucid assessment of Gracchus' career.

P. A. L. Greenhalgh, *Pompey*, 2 vols. (London, 1980, 1981). The first volume, *The Roman Alexander,* covers Pompey's career down to 59 B.C.; the second, *The Republican Prince*, the period of his ascendancy.

E. S. Gruen, *The Last Generation of the Roman Republic* (Berkeley, 1974). Erudite and controversial analysis of the post-Sullan period.

A. Keaveney, *Sulla: The Last Republican* (London, 1982). The most thorough treatment in English, but not entirely convincing in its attempt to portray Sulla as greatly misunderstood.

C. Meier, *Caesar* (New York, 1995). Readable, if undocumented, biography of Caesar that also addresses many aspects of Late Republican politics and society.

D. Stockton, *The Gracchi* (Oxford, 1979). Readable survey of the main issues surrounding these men and one of the only serious modern studies of Gaius Gracchus.

E. Rawson, *Cicero: A Portrait* (Ithaca, 1975). A thorough biography of Cicero by a leading historian of the Republic.

J. M. Riddle, (comp.), *Tiberius Gracchus: Destroyer or Reformer of the Republic?* (Lexington, Mass., 1970). Handy collection of ancient sources and modern discussions of this important figure.

R. Seager, *Pompey: A Political Biography* (Oxford, 1979). An eminently sane and thoroughly documented account.

R. Syme, *The Roman Revolution* (Oxford, 1939). A seminal work, casting the machinations of Augustus in a distinctly dictatorial light, as suited to the age in which Syme was writing.

A. M. Ward, *Marcus Crassus and the Late Roman Republic* (Columbia, MO, 1977). A well-documented survey.

Augustus and the Emperors:

M. Grant, *The Roman Emperors: A Biographical Guide to the Rulers of Imperial Rome, 31 B.C.–A.D. 476* (New York, 1985). A short dictionary of Roman emperors, arranged chronologically; contains a useful glossary of ancient literary evidence at the back.

R. A. Gurval, *Actium and Augustus: The Politics and Emotions of Civil War* (Ann Arbor, 1995). An interesting and sustained analysis of how contemporaries reacted to the victory at Actium and how the commemoration of the battle evolved over time.

A. H. M. Jones, *Augustus* (London, 1970). A sensible and reliable outline account of Augustus' reign.

F. Millar, *The Emperor in the Roman World* (London, 1977). A massive and masterful, if unabashedly positivistic, study of the subject that puts forward the view that "the emperor was what the emperor did."

K. A. Raaflaub and M. Toher, eds., *Between Republic and Empire: Interpretations of Augustus and His Principate* (Berkeley, 1990). A collection of nineteen essays by respected scholars on various aspects of Augustus' career; requires some basic knowledge to be used profitably.

D. Shotter, *Augustus Caesar* (London, 1991). A short and recent introduction to Augustus' career that covers all the issues and has useful pointers for further reading.

Readers are also directed to individual biographies of emperors, easily traceable by their names, and to the Internet site *De Imperatoribus Romanis: An Online Encyclopedia of Roman Emperors*; the site includes specific bibliographies for each entry (http://www.salve.edu/~dimaio/deimprom.html).

Third Century and Late Empire:

G. C. Brauer, *The Age of the Soldier-Emperors: Imperial Rome, A.D. 244–84* (Park Ridge, NJ, 1975). A very general overview of the darkest period of Rome's third-century crisis.

P. Brown, *The World of Late Antiquity, A.D. 150–750* (London, 1971). A fine exposition of the "Transformationist" view of the Late Empire

A. Cameron, *The Mediterranean World in Late Antiquity, A.D. 395– 600* (New York, 1993). An excellent overview of the Late Empire from Theodosius to Justinian's Reconquest.

A. H. M. Jones, *The Later Roman Empire, 284–602* (Oxford, 1964; reprinted Baltimore, 1986). The standard, monumental and magisterial two-volume treatment of the Late Empire.

R. Stoneman, *Palmyra and its Empire* (Ann Arbor, 1992). In examining the rise and fall of Zenobia and the breakaway Palmyran state, the author explores some of the salient features of the third-century crisis.

S. Williams, *Diocletian and the Roman Recovery* (London, 1985). An examination of Diocletian's pivotal reign in reestablishing order to the Roman world.

Aspects of Roman Culture and Society:

J. C. Anderson, Jr., *Roman Architecture and Society* (Baltimore, 1997). A recent survey of Roman buildings and their relationship to daily life.

J. P. V. D. Balsdon, *Life and Leisure in Ancient Rome* (London, 1969). A classic treatment of the subject with rich documentation from a variety of obscure ancient sources.

A. A. Barrett, *Agrippina: Sex, Power, and Politics in the Early Empire* (New Haven, 1996). The life of one of Roman history's most powerful and intriguing women is thoroughly investigated.

A. Boethius, *Etruscan and Early Roman Architecture*, 2nd edition (London, 1978). A standard work on the subject.

R. Bradley, *Discovering the Roman Family* (Oxford, 1991). An insightful and stimulating study of the nature of the Roman family unit.

——————, *Slavery and Society at Rome* (Cambridge, 1994). A superlative consideration of the condition of slavery in ancient Rome.

L. A. Curchin, *The Local Magistrates of Roman Spain* (Toronto, 1990). Despite the dry title, the book offers an excellent window onto municipal administration and politics.

S. Dixon, *The Roman Family* (Baltimore, 1992). A thorough introduction to the study of the subject.

G. G. Fagan, *Bathing in Public in the Roman World* (Ann Arbor, 1999). This book approaches the baths as historical, cultural, and social phenomena and so throws light on the daily operation of Roman society.

E. Fantham, H. P. Foley, N. B. Kampen, S. B. Pomeroy, H. A. Shapiro, *Women in the Classical World* (Oxford, 1994). Generally sound survey of the position of women in classical antiquity; the second part focuses on Roman women.

M. I. Finley, *Ancient Slavery and Modern Ideology* (London, 1980). A seminal work in the field, deploying much comparative and theoretical data in approaching ancient slavery.

R. L. Fox, *Pagans and Christians* (New York, 1987). A lengthy study of the Christian conflict with paganism up to the death of Constantine.

W. H. C. Frend, *The Rise of Christianity* (Philadelphia, 1984). A standard, monumental treatment of Christianity's early history that covers the Jewish background, the life of Jesus, internal Christian disputes, and the conflict with paganism.

A. Futrell, *Blood in the Arena: The Spectacle of Roman Power* (Austin, 1997). A novel treatment of the games as mass human sacrifices reinforcing the reality of Roman power.

*P. Garnsey and R. Saller, *The Roman Empire: Economy, Society, Culture* (Berkeley, 1987). A sane introductory presentation of various aspects of Roman life from two leading scholars.

D. G. Kyle, *Spectacles of Death in Ancient Rome* (London, 1998). Rejecting the "rebirth" interpretation of the games (see under Wiedemann, below), this fascinating and often gruesome study highlights the scale of death and suffering in the arena as ritualized maintenance of the social and religious order

A. Lintott, Imperium Romanum: *Politics and Administration* (London, 1993). Survey of the administration of the Roman state and empire.

R. MacMullen, *Paganism in the Roman Empire* (New Haven, 1981). An excellent introduction to the main principles and practices of paganism.

—————, *Roman Social Relations, 50 B.C. to A.D. 284* (New Haven, 1984). A thoughtful and well-written assessment of the life of the much-neglected Roman lower classes.

R. M. Ogilvie, *The Romans and Their Gods* (London, 1969). An elegantly concise and masterful portrait of Roman paganism.

P. Plass, *The Game of Death in Ancient Rome: Arena Sport and Political Suicide* (Madison, 1995). An anthropological analysis of the arena as a "liminoid ritual" that harnessed and neutralized potentially destructive forces in society.

J. E. Stambaugh, *The Ancient Roman City* (Baltimore, 1988). A clear introduction to the physicality of and living conditions in Roman urban centers.

J. P. Toner, *Leisure and Ancient Rome* (Cambridge, 1995). Although the most recent survey of the subject available in English, the treatment suffers from a somewhat overdependency on theoretical approaches.

*T. Wiedemann, *Emperors and Gladiators* (London, 1992). A stimulating read that describes all the elements in the Roman gladiatorial spectacle and argues for an interpretation of the games as metaphors of rebirth.

R. L. Wilken, *The Christians as the Romans Saw Them* (New Haven, 1984). An insightful book that makes comprehensible the vices of the Christian faith, as seen through pagan eyes.

F. Yegül, *Baths and Bathing in Classical Antiquity* (Cambridge, MA, 1992). A comprehensive treatment of the architectural and technological development of the Roman bath with many useful cultural and social insights.

End of Empire:

A. Ferrill, *The Fall of the Roman Empire: The Military Explanation* (London, 1986). A narrowly focused study arguing that Rome's military inability to withstand barbarian invasions caused its fall.

J. D. Hughes. *Pan's Travail: Environmental Problems of the Ancient Greek and Romans* (Baltimore, 1994). An idealistic presentation of the environmental explanation for the end of the ancient world in the west.

D. Kagan, ed., *The End of the Roman Empire* (Lexington, MA, 1992). A useful assemblage of ancient and modern views of the fall of the Roman Empire in the west.

R. MacMullen, *Corruption and the Decline of Rome* (New Haven, 1988). An excellent example of carefully argued, well-documented, and engagingly written "general" explanation for Rome's fall.